Edward Griffin Tileston

Handbook of the administrations of the United States

Edward Griffin Tileston

Handbook of the administrations of the United States

ISBN/EAN: 9783337132262

Printed in Europe, USA, Canada, Australia, Japan

Cover: Foto ©Suzi / pixelio.de

More available books at **www.hansebooks.com**

Tileston's Hand-Book.

HANDBOOK

OF THE

ADMINISTRATIONS

OF THE

UNITED STATES;

COMPRISING A SYNOPSIS OF THE LEADING POLITICAL
EVENTS IN AMERICAN HISTORY, FROM THE
INAUGURATION OF WASHINGTON TO
THE PRESENT PERIOD.

ALSO A

RECORD OF CONTEMPORANEOUS ENGLISH HISTORY.

By EDWARD G. TILESTON.

BOSTON:
LEE & SHEPARD, PUBLISHERS.
NEW YORK:
LEE, SHEPARD, AND DILLINGHAM.
1871.

Entered, according to Act of Congress, in the year 1870,
By EDWARD G. TILESTON, LL.B.,
In the Office of the Librarian of Congress, at Washington.

Boston:
Stereotyped and Printed by Rand, Avery, & Frye.

PREFACE.

A FEW months ago, passing through the library of the Boston Athenæum, we picked up a "Handbook of the Administrations of Great Britain," written by Francis Culling Carr, Esq.; published by Smith, Elder, & Co., London. The thought at once occurred to us, that a Handbook of the Administrations of the United States would also be a valuable manual. This little volume is the result. Nothing elaborate is intended. It is simply a collection of familiar facts carefully grouped together in moments of leisure from business engagements, — facts so classified and arranged as to be easily remembered, and readily referred to. Notwithstanding the limits of the work, we have given extended extracts from the inaugural and other addresses of the early Presidents; also leading incidents in contemporaneous English and French history, and official financial statements of the General Government. Although the Vice-President of the United States is not a member of the cabinet, and the Postmaster-General was not admitted until Jackson's time, we have thought best to give the names of these officers with those who actually belong to that body. We are indebted to the courtesy of the Superintendent of the Department of the Interior, Washington, for the facts in the Appendix, "Census 1870," which have been kindly furnished in advance of the official publication. As it is not impossible that a new edition of this Handbook may be issued at the close of each administration, suggestions are respectfully requested for its improvement, and may be addressed to the Editor.

Boston, March 4, 1871.

WASHINGTON'S ADMINISTRATION.

1789 TO 1797.

THE CABINET.

PRESIDENT:
GEORGE WASHINGTON, Virginia.
VICE-PRESIDENT:
JOHN ADAMS, Massachusetts.

SECRETARIES OF STATE:
1789. — Thomas Jefferson, Virginia.
1794. — Edmund Randolph, Virginia.
1795. — Timothy Pickering, Massachusetts.

SECRETARIES OF THE TREASURY:
1789. — Alexander Hamilton, New York.
1795. — Oliver Wolcott, Connecticut.

SECRETARIES OF WAR AND NAVY:
1789. — Henry Knox, Massachusetts.
1794. — Timothy Pickering, Massachusetts.
1796. — James McHenry, Maryland.

POSTMASTERS-GENERAL:
1789. — Samuel Osgood, Massachusetts.
1794. — Timothy Pickering, Massachusetts.
1795. — Joseph Habersham, Georgia.

ATTORNEYS-GENERAL:
1789. — Edmund Randolph, Virginia.
1794. — William Bradford, Pennsylvania.
1795. — Charles Lee, Virginia.

CONTEMPORANEOUS ENGLISH HISTORY.

George III., King of England.
Mr. Pitt, Prime-Minister.
Revolution in France, and }
War between France and England; }
Napoleon First Consul. }

GEORGE WASHINGTON.

FROM — March 4, 1789, to 1797.
DURATION. — Two terms, — eight years.
PARTY. — Federalists.
PRINCIPAL EVENTS. — Organization of the Federal Government. National Thanksgiving established. United States Bank organized. Federal loan negotiated in Europe. Land secured for seat of government. Death of Franklin at 84. North Carolina, Vermont, Tennessee, and Kentucky admitted. Indian hostilities. Whiskey Insurrection. Subsequent prosperity. Farewell Address.
PRESIDENT OF SENATE. — John Adams.
CHAPLAIN OF SENATE, 1789. — Rt. Rev. Bishop Provost (Episcopal).
SPEAKERS OF THE HOUSE. — First Congress, F. A. Muhlenberg, Pennsylvania.
Second Congress, Jonathan Trumbull, Connecticut.
Third Congress, F. A. Muhlenberg, Pennsylvania.
Fourth Congress, Jonathan Dayton, New Jersey.
CHAPLAIN OF HOUSE, 1789. — Rev. William Lynn (Presbyterian).
CHANCELLOR OF NEW YORK. — Robert R. Livingston.

1789. — The first marked event in the administration of Washington was his reception by Congress, convened in New York.

His journey from Mount Vernon had been like a triumphal procession, the way often strewed with flowers.

Addresses, both public and private, were aglow with gratitude to the Father of his Country, but, above all, to Almighty God, who had raised him up to be a nation's deliverer.

It was just prior to this reception that John Adams said of him, "Were I blessed with powers to do justice to his character, it would be impossible to increase the confidence or affection of his country, or make the smallest addition to his glory. If we look over the catalogue of the first magistrates of nations, whether they have been denominated presidents or consuls, kings or princes, where shall we find one whose commanding talents and virtues, whose overruling good fortune, have so completely united all hearts and voices in his favor, who enjoyed the esteem and admiration of foreign nations and fellow-citizens with equal unanimity? Qualities so uncommon are no common blessings to the country that possesses them. By these great qualities and their benign effects has Providence marked out the head of this nation with a hand so distinctly visible as to have been seen by all men, and mistaken by none." And Washington in his Inaugural Address remarked, " It would be peculiarly improper to omit in this my first official act my fervent supplications to that Almighty Being who rules over the universe, who presides in the councils of nations, and whose providential aid can supply every human defect that his benediction may consecrate to the liberties and happiness of the people of the United States." And again : "No people can be bound to acknowledge and adore the invisible Hand which conducts the affairs of men more than the people of the United States. The propitious smiles of Heaven can never be expected on a nation that disregards the eternal rules of order and right, which Heaven itself has ordained. The preservation of the sacred fire of liberty, and the creating of the Republican model of government, are justly considered as deeply, perhaps as finally, staked on the experiment intrusted to the hands of the American people." To which the Senate, among other excellent things, replied, " We rejoice, and with us all America, that, in obedience to the call of our common country, you have returned once more to public life. In you all parties confide; in you all interests unite. A review of the many signal instances of divine interposition in favor of this country claims our most pious gratitude; and permit us, sir, to observe, that, among the great events which have led to the formation and establishment of a Federal Government, we esteem your acceptance of the office of President as one of the most propitious and important." The answer of the House was in part as follows: "We feel, with you, the strongest obligations to adore the invisible Hand which has led the American people through so many difficulties; to cherish a conscious responsibility for the destiny of Republican liberty; and to seek the only sure means of preserving and recommending the precious deposit in a system of legislation founded on the principles of an honest policy, and directed by the spirit of a diffusive patriotism. Your resolution, in a moment critical to the liberties of your country, to renounce all personal emolument, was among the many presages of your patriotic services which have been amply fulfilled; and your scrupulous adherence now to the law then imposed on yourself cannot fail to demonstrate the purity, whilst it increases the lustre, of a character which has so many titles to admiration. Such are the sentiments which we have thought fit to address you. They flow from our hearts; and we verily believe, that, among the millions we represent, there is not a virtuous citizen whose heart will disown them." A part of the reply of the beloved Washington was this: "I now feel myself inexpressibly happy in a belief that Heaven, which has done so much for an infant nation, will not withdraw its providential influence before our political felicity shall have been completed. Thus supported by a firm trust in the great Arbiter of the universe, aided by the collective wisdom of the Union, and imploring the divine benediction on our joint exertions in the service of our country, I readily engage with you in the arduous but pleasing task of attempting to make a nation happy."

Previously to the adjournment of the first session of Congress, the two houses appointed a joint committee to wait on the President to "request that he would recommend to the people of the United States a day of public thanksgiving and prayer, to be observed by acknowledging with grateful hearts the many and signal favors of Almighty God; especially by affording them an opportunity peaceably to establish a constitution of government for their safety and happiness."

1790.—The second session of the first Congress assembled in New York on Monday, the 4th of January. Washington congratulates the country upon the "recent accession of the important State of North Carolina;" advises with regard to certain hostile tribes of Indians, post-offices, and post-roads; uniformity in the currency, weights, and measures; the advancement of agriculture, commerce, and manufactures; the promotion of science and literature, and an adequate provision for the support of the public credit; the department of foreign affairs; and a uniform rule of naturalization, by which foreigners may be admitted to the rights of citizens.

1791.—The third session of the first Congress was assembled at the county court house in the city of Philadelphia. At this session, the whole of the thirteen States were represented. Washington alludes to the rise of American securities abroad, as well as at home; recommends the appointment of foreign consuls; speaks of the disturbed situation of Europe, and advises the establishment of the militia for the protection of the frontiers; Vermont is admitted to the Union; "public debt to be reduced as fast as the increase of the public resources will permit;" a loan of three millions of florins is negotiated in Holland.

1791-92.—Second Congress, first session. Philadelphia, 24th October, 1791. Rapid subscriptions to the Bank of the United States; overtures of peace accepted by certain Indian tribes; a district of ten miles square for the permanent seat of government of the United States is fixed, and announced by proclamation, which district comprehends land on both sides of the River Potomac, and the towns of Alexandria and Georgetown; population of United States, four millions; a further loan of two millions and a half of florins completed in Holland; six millions more expected; arsenals, fortifications, and a mint, to be established; United States lands pledged as a fund for reimbursing the public debt; Kentucky admitted into the Union.

1792-93.—Second Congress, second session. Philadelphia, 5th November, 1792.

Financial prosperity continues. Three new loans effected, each for three millions of florins, at Antwerp and Amsterdam, at four per cent. Efforts to establish peace with hostile Indians unavailing.

Washington opens his address to Congress thus:—

"I entertain a strong hope that the state of the national finances is now sufficiently matured to enable you to enter upon a systematic and effectual arrangement for the regular redemption and discharge of the public debt. No measure can be more desirable, whether viewed with an eye to its intrinsic importance, or to the general sentiment and wish of the nation."

Soon after entering upon his second term, Washington says, "I have obeyed the suffrage which commanded me to resume the executive power; and I humbly implore that Being, on whose will the fate of nations depends, to crown with success our mutual endeavors for the general happiness."

1794.—"The mint of the United States has

entered upon the coinage of the precious metals. My policy in our foreign transactions has been, to cultivate peace with all the world; to observe treaties with pure and absolute faith; to check every deviation from the line of impartiality; to explain what may have been misapprehended, and correct what may have been injurious to any nation; and having thus acquired the right, to lose no time in acquiring the ability, to insist upon justice being done to ourselves. Let us unite, therefore, in imploring the Supreme Ruler of nations to spread his holy protection over these United States; to turn the machinations of the wicked to the confirming of our Constitution; to enable us at all times to root out internal sedition, and put invasion to flight; to perpetuate to our country that prosperity which his goodness has already conferred; and to verify the anticipations of this government being a safeguard to human rights."

1794.—November. To Congress: "When we call to mind the gracious indulgence of Heaven, by which the American people became a nation; when we survey the general prosperity of our country, and look forward to the riches, power, and happiness to which it seems destined, — with the deepest regret do I announce to you, that, during your recess, some of the citizens of the United States have been found capable of an insurrection; ... to withstand by force of arms the authority of the United States, and thereby to extort a repeal of the law of excise, and an alteration in the conduct of government. ... I therefore entertain a hope that the present session will not pass without carrying to its fullest energy the power of organizing, arming, and disciplining the militia; and thus providing, in the language of the Constitution, for calling them forth to execute the laws of the Union, suppress insurrections, and repel invasion." Respecting the Indians, he says, "Towards none of the Indian tribes have overtures of friendship been spared."

1795. — Dec. 8. "I trust I do not deceive myself while I indulge the persuasion that I have never met you at any period, when, more than at the present, the situation of our public affairs has afforded just cause for mutual congratulation, and for inviting you to join with me in profound gratitude to the Author of all good for the numerous and extraordinary blessings we enjoy. . . . A treaty of amity, commerce, and navigation, has been negotiated with Great Britain. . . . Every part of the Union displays indications of rapid and various improvement; and with burdens so light as scarcely to be perceived, with resources fully adequate to our present exigencies, with governments founded on the genuine principles of rational liberty, and with mild and wholesome laws, is it too much to say that our country exhibits a spectacle of national happiness never surpassed, if ever before equalled? It is a valuable ingredient in the general estimate of our welfare, that the part of our country which was lately the scene of disorder and insurrection now enjoys the blessings of quiet and order. These circumstances have induced me to pardon, generally, the offenders here referred to, and to extend forgiveness to those who have been adjudged to capital punishment."

1796. — Dec. 7. "I find ample reason for a renewed expression of that gratitude to the Ruler of the universe which a continued series of prosperity has so often and so justly called forth."

Respecting the creation of a navy, Washington says, "To an active external commerce the protection of a naval force is indispensable. This is manifest with regard to wars in which a State is itself a party. But, besides this, it is in our experience that the most sincere neutrality is not a sufficient guard against the depredations of nations at war. To secure respect to a neutral flag requires a naval force, organized, and ready to vindicate it from insult or aggression: this may even prevent the necessity of going to war. . . . I trust a future war with Europe may not find our commerce in the same unprotected state in which it was found by the present."

Of manufactures, "Congress have repeatedly, and not without success, directed their attention to the encouragement of manufactures. The object is of too much consequence not to insure a continuance of their efforts." And of agriculture, "It will not be doubted, that, with reference either to individual or national welfare, agriculture is of primary importance: institutions for promoting it grow up supported by the public purse; and to what object can it be dedicated with greater propriety? ... Experience has shown that these institutions are very cheap instruments of immense national benefits. ... I have heretofore proposed to the consideration of Congress the expediency of establishing a national university, and also a military academy.... The assembly to which I address myself is too enlightened not to be fully sensible how much a flourishing state of the arts and sciences contributes to national prosperity and reputation. The common education of a portion of our youth from every quarter deserves attention. The more homogeneous our citizens can be made in these particulars, the greater will be our prospect of permanent union; and a primary object of such a national institution should be the education of our youth in the science of *government*. In a republic, what species of knowledge can be equally important? and what duty more pressing on its legislature than to patronize a plan for communicating it to those who are to be the future guardians of the liberties of the country? ... However pacific the general policy of a nation may be, it ought never to be without an adequate stock of military knowledge for emergencies.... An academy where a regular course of instruction is given is an obvious expedient, which different nations have successfully employed. . . . The compensations to the officers of the United States appear to call for legislative revision. It would be repugnant to the vital principles of our government virtually to exclude from public trusts talents and virtues unless accompanied by wealth." Of the French Republic he says, " It has been my constant, sincere, and earnest wish, in conformity with that of our nation, to maintain cordial harmony and a perfectly friendly understanding with the Republic. This wish remains unabated; and I shall persevere in the endeavor to fulfil it to the utmost extent of what shall be consistent with a just and indispensable regard to the rights and honor of our country. Nor will I easily cease to cherish the expectation, that a spirit of justice, candor, and friendship, on the part of the Republic, will eventually insure success." Respecting the speedy extinguishment of the United States debt, he says, " Posterity may have cause to regret, if, from any motive, intervals of tranquillity are left unimproved for accelerating this valuable end."

1797. — The following is the closing language of Washington's last Annual Address to Congress: —

"The situation in which I now stand for the last time, in the midst of the representatives of the people of the United States, naturally recalls the period when the administration of the present form of government commenced; and I cannot omit the occasion to congratulate you and my country on the success of the experiment, nor to repeat my fervent supplications to the Supreme Ruler of the universe, and Sovereign Arbiter of nations, that his providential care may still be extended to the United States, that the virtue and happiness of the people may be preserved, and that the government which they have instituted for the protection of their liberties may be perpetual."

Upon the occasion of his retirement, he issued his Farewell Address to the people of the United States, embodying the results of his experience and observation during a long career of public service devoted to the highest interests of his country. From this address we here present several extracts: —

"Of all the dispositions and habits which lead to political prosperity, religion and morality are indispensable supports. In vain would that man claim the tribute of patriotism, who should labor to subvert these great pillars of human happiness, these firmest props of the duties of men and citizens. The mere politician, equally with the pious man, ought to respect and to cherish them. A volume could not trace all their connections with private and public felicity. Reason and experience both forbid us to expect that national morality can prevail in exclusion of religious principle. . . . Observe good faith and justice towards all nations; cultivate peace and harmony with all. Religion and morality enjoin this conduct; and can it be that good policy does not equally enjoin it? Can it be that Providence has not connected the permanent felicity of a nation with its virtue? . . . The great rule of conduct for us, in regard to foreign nations, is, in extending our commercial relations, to have with them as little political connection as possible. So far as we have already formed engagements, let them be fulfilled with perfect good faith. Here let us stop. . . . Harmony, and a liberal intercourse with all nations, are recommended by policy, humanity, and interest. But even our commercial policy should hold an equal and impartial hand; neither seeking nor granting exclusive favors or preferences; consulting the natural course of things; diffusing and diversifying by gentle means the streams of commerce, but forcing nothing; constantly keeping in view that it is folly in one nation to look for disinterested favors from another; that it must pay with a portion of its independence for whatever it may accept under that character; that by such acceptance it may place itself in the condition of having given equivalents for nominal favors, and yet of being reproached with ingratitude for not giving more. There can be no greater error than to expect or calculate upon real favors from nation to nation. 'Tis all illusion, which experience must cure, which a just pride ought to discard. . . . The nation which indulges towards another an habitual hatred or an habitual fondness, is, in some degree, a slave: it is a slave to its animosity or to its affection, either of which is sufficient to lead it astray from its duty and its interest. . . . Citizens, by birth or choice, of a common country, that country has a right to concentrate your affections. The North, in an unrestrained intercourse with the South, protected by the equal laws of a common government, finds in the productions of the latter great additional resources of maritime and commercial enterprise, and precious materials of manufacturing industry. The South, in the same intercourse, benefiting by the agency of the North, sees its agriculture grow, and its commerce expand. Turning partly into its own channels the seamen of the North, it finds its particular navigation invigorated; and, while it contributes in different ways to nourish and increase the general mass of the national navigation, it looks forward to the protection of a maritime strength.

"The East, in like intercourse with the West, already finds, and, in the progressive improvement of interior communication by land and water, will more and more find, a valuable vent for the commodities which it brings from abroad, or manufactures at home. The West derives from the East supplies requisite to its growth and comfort; and what is, perhaps, of still greater consequence, it must, of necessity, owe the secure enjoyment of indispensable outlets for its own productions to the weight, influence, and the future maritime strength, of the Atlantic side of the Union, directed by an indissoluble community of interest as one nation.

"In offering to you, my countrymen, these counsels of an old and affectionate friend, I dare not hope they will make the strong and lasting impression I could wish ; that they will control the usual current of the passions, or prevent our nation from running the course which has hitherto marked the destiny of nations: but if I may even flatter myself that they may be productive of some partial benefit, some occasional good ; that they may now and then recur to moderate the fury of party spirit, to warn against the mischiefs of foreign intrigue, to guard against the impostures of pretended patriotism, — this hope will be a full recompense for the solicitude for your welfare by which they have been dictated.

"Though, in reviewing the incidents of my administration, I am unconscious of intentional error, I am, nevertheless, too sensible of my defects not to think it probable that I may have committed many errors. Whatever they may be, I fervently beseech the Almighty to avert or mitigate the evils to which they may tend. I shall also carry with me the hope, that my country will never cease to view them with indulgence; and that, after forty-five years of my life dedicated to its service with an upright zeal, the faults of incompetent abilities will be consigned to oblivion, as myself must soon be to the mansions of rest.

"GEORGE WASHINGTON."

At the close of Washington's administration, the Federalists nominated John Adams for President; and the Republicans, Thomas Jefferson: and Adams was elected by two electoral votes.

JOHN ADAMS'S ADMINISTRATION.

1797 TO 1801.

THE CABINET.

PRESIDENT:
JOHN ADAMS, Massachusetts.
VICE-PRESIDENT:
THOMAS JEFFERSON, Virginia.

SECRETARIES OF STATE:
1797. — Timothy Pickering, Massachusetts.
1800. — John Marshall, Virginia.

SECRETARIES OF THE TREASURY:
1797. — Oliver Wolcott, Connecticut.
1800. — S. Dexter, Massachusetts.

SECRETARIES OF WAR:
1797. — James McHenry, Maryland.
1800 — S. Dexter, Massachusetts.
1801. — Roger Griswold, Connecticut.

SECRETARIES OF THE NAVY:
1798. — George Cabot, Massachusetts (declined).
1798. — Benjamin Stoddert, Maryland

POSTMASTER-GENERAL:
1797. — Joseph Habersham, Georgia.

ATTORNEY-GENERAL:
1797. — Charles Lee, Virginia.

CONTEMPORANEOUS ENGLISH HISTORY.

George III., King of England.
Mr. Pitt, Prime-Minister.
First Imperial Parliament of the Union of Great Britain and Ireland.
French War, since 1793, still raging.
Napoleon First Consul of France.

JOHN ADAMS.

FROM — 1797 to 1801.
DURATION. — One term, — four years.
PARTY. — Federalists.
PRINCIPAL EVENTS. — War threatened by France on account of Jay's treaty with England. American vessels captured by French cruisers. Envoys insulted in Paris. French officials expect a bribe. Pinckney replies to Talleyrand, "Millions for defence, but not one cent for tribute." Congress decides to raise an army. Washington re-appointed commander-in-chief. Navy created in 1798. Seat of government established in the District of Columbia. Differences between Adams and Hamilton. Adams and the Federalists bitterly opposed by Jefferson and the Republicans on account of the " alien * and sedition laws " against rebel aliens and government libellers. Death of Washington at Mt. Vernon, Dec. 14, 1799. Treaty negotiated with Napoleon Bonaparte in 1800. Downfall of Federalism. Election of Jefferson by the Republican State sovereignty, or Democratic party.

1797. — March 4. The Inaugural Address of Adams opens as follows: "When it was first per-

---

* "If Jefferson and Madison deemed the Alien and Sedition Acts plain and palpable infractions of the Constitution, Washington and Patrick Henry held them to be good and wholesome laws." — *John Quincy Adams.*

ceived, in early times, that no middle course for America remained between unlimited submission to a foreign legislature and a total independence of its claims, men of reflection were less apprehensive of danger from the formidable power of fleets and armies they must determine to resist than from those contests and dissensions which would certainly arise, concerning the forms of governments to be instituted over the whole and over the parts of this extensive country. Relying, however, on the purity of their intentions, the justice of their cause, and the integrity and intelligence of the people, under an overruling Providence, which had so signally protected this country from the first, the representatives of this nation, then consisting of little more than half its present numbers, not only broke to pieces the chains which were forging, and the rod of iron that was lifted up, but frankly cut asunder the ties which had bound them, and launched into an ocean of uncertainty." Alluding briefly to the zeal and ardor of the people during the Revolutionary War, and the organization of a confederation resulting in the Federal Constitution, he continues: "Employed in the service of my country abroad during the whole course of these transactions, I first saw the Constitution of the United States in a foreign country. Irritated by no literary altercation, animated by no public debate, heated by no party animosity, I read it with great satisfaction, as a result of good heads prompted by good hearts; as an experiment better adapted to the genius, character, situation, and relations of this nation and country than any which had ever been proposed or suggested. Returning to the bosom of my country after a painful separation from it for ten years, I had the honor to be elected to a station under the new order of things; and I have repeatedly laid myself under the most serious obligations to support the Constitution. The operation of it has equalled the most sanguine expectations of its friends; and from an habitual attention to it, satisfaction in its administration, and delight in its effects upon the peace, order, prosperity, and happiness of the nation, I have acquired an habitual attachment to it, and veneration for it. What other form of government, indeed, can so well deserve our esteem and love?"

May 17. — "It would have afforded me the highest satisfaction to have been able to congratulate you on a restoration of peace to the nations of Europe, whose animosities have endangered our tranquillity; but we have still abundant cause of gratitude to the Supreme Dispenser of national blessings, for general health and promising seasons, for domestic and social happiness, for the rapid progress and ample acquisitions of industry through extensive territories, for civil, political, and religious liberty. While other States are desolated with foreign war, or convulsed with intestine divisions, the United States presented the pleasing prospect of a nation governed by mild and equal laws, generally satisfied with the possession of their rights; neither envying the advantages, nor fearing the power, of other nations; yielding a ready and general obedience to laws flowing from the reason, and resting on the only solid foundation, — the affections of the people. It is with extreme regret that I shall be obliged to turn your thoughts to other circumstances, which admonish us that some of these felicities may not be lasting. . . .

"A few days before his arrival at Paris, the French minister of foreign affairs informed the American minister, then resident at Paris, of the formalities to be observed by himself in taking leave, and by his successor preparatory to his reception. These formalities they observed, and, on the 9th of December, presented officially to the minister of foreign relations, — the one, a copy of his letter of recall; the other, a copy of his letter of credence: these were laid before the Executive Directory. Two days afterwards, the minister of foreign relations informed the recalled American minister that the Executive Directory had determined not to receive another minister-plenipotentiary from the United States until after the redress of grievances demanded of the American Government, and which the French republic had a right to expect from it. The American minister immediately endeavored to ascertain whether, by refusing to receive him, it was intended that he should retire from the territories of the French republic; and verbal answers were given, that such was the intention of the Directory. For his own justification he desired a written answer, but obtained none.

until towards the last of January; when, receiving notice, in writing, to quit the territories of the republic, he proceeded to Amsterdam, where he proposed to wait for instructions from his government. During his residence at Paris, cards of hospitality were refused him, and he was threatened with being subjected to the jurisdiction of the minister of police; but with becoming firmness he insisted on the protection of the law of nations due to him as the known minister of a foreign power. The speech of the president discloses sentiments more alarming than the refusal of a minister, because more dangerous to our independence and union, and at the same time studiously marked with indignities towards the government of the United States. It evinces a disposition to separate the people of the United States from the government; to persuade them that they have different affections, principles, and interests from those of their fellow-citizens whom they themselves have chosen to manage their common concerns; and thus to produce divisions fatal to our peace. I should have been happy to have thrown a veil over these transactions, if it had been possible to conceal them; but they have passed on the great theatre of the world in the face of all Europe and America, and with such circumstances of publicity and solemnity, that they cannot be disguised, and will not soon be forgotten. They have inflicted a wound in the American breast: it is my sincere desire, however, that it may be healed. It is my desire, and in this I presume I concur with you and with our constituents, to preserve peace and friendship with all nations; and, believing that neither the honor nor the interest of the United States absolutely forbids the repetition of advances for securing these desirable objects with France, I shall institute a fresh attempt at negotiation, and shall not fail to promote and accelerate an accommodation on terms compatible with the rights, duties, interests, and honor of the nation. If we have committed errors, and these can be demonstrated, we shall be willing to correct them; if we have done injuries, we shall be willing, on conviction, to redress them: and equal measures of justice we have a right to expect from France and every other nation. While we are endeavoring to adjust all our differences with France by amicable negotiation, the progress of the war in Europe, the depredations on our commerce, the personal injuries to our citizens, and the general complexion of affairs, render it my indispensable duty to recommend to your consideration effectual measures of defence. With a seacoast of near two thousand miles in extent, opening a wide field for fisheries, navigation, and commerce, a great portion of our citizens naturally apply their industry and enterprise to these objects. Any serious and permanent injury to commerce would not fail to produce the most embarrassing disorders: to prevent it from being undermined and destroyed, it is essential that it receive an adequate protection. A naval power, next to the militia, is the natural defence of the United States. However we may consider ourselves, the maritime and commercial powers of the world will consider the United States of America as forming a weight in that balance of power in Europe which never can be forgotten or neglected. . . . It is impossible to conceal from ourselves or the world that endeavors have been employed to foster and establish a division between the government and the people of the United States. To investigate the causes which have encouraged this attempt is not necessary; but to repel by decided and united councils insinuations so derogatory to the honor, and aggressions so dangerous to the constitution, union, and even independence, of the nation, is an indispensable duty. It must not be permitted to be doubted whether the people of the United States will support the government established by their voluntary consent, and appointed by their free choice; or whether, by surrendering themselves to the direction of foreign and domestic factions, in opposition to their own government, they will forfeit the honorable station they have hitherto maintained."

Nov. 23. — "Although I cannot yet congratulate you on the re-establishment of peace in Europe, and the restoration of security to the persons and properties of our citizens from injustice and violence at sea, we have, nevertheless, abundant causes of gratitude to the Source of benevolence and influence for interior tranquillity and personal security; for propitious seasons, prosperous agriculture, productive fisheries, and general improvements; and, above all, for a rational spirit of civil and religious liberty, and a calm but steady determination to support our sovereignty as well as our moral and religious principles against all open and secret attacks. Our envoys-extraordinary to the French republic embarked, one in July, the other early in August, to join their colleague in Holland. I have received intelligence of the arrival of both of them in Holland, from whence they all proceeded on their journeys to Paris. Several decisions on the claims of citizens of the United States for losses and damages sustained by reason of irregular and illegal captures have been made by the commissioners in London, conformable to the seventh article of the treaty. The sums awarded by the commissioners have been paid by the British Government. A considerable number of other claims, where costs and damages, and not captured property, were the only objects in question, have been decided by arbitration; and the sums awarded to the citizens of the United States have also been paid."

1798.— Dec. 8. "The United States will steadily observe the maxims by which they have hitherto been governed. They will respect the sacred rights of embassy; and with a sincere disposition on the part of France to desist from hostility, to make reparation for the injuries heretofore inflicted on our commerce, and to do justice in future, there will be no obstacle to the restoration of a friendly intercourse. I give a pledge to France and to the world, that the executive authority of this country still adheres to the humane and pacific policy which has invariably governed its proceedings in conformity with the wishes of the other branches of the government and of the people of the United States. Harmony between us and France may be restored at her option."

1799. — Dec. 3. "The flattering prospects of abundance from the labors of the people by land and by sea; the prosperity of our extended commerce, notwithstanding interruptions occasioned by the belligerent state of a great part of the world; the return of health, industry, and trade to those cities which have lately been afflicted with disease; and the various and inestimable advantages, civil and religious, which, secured under our happy frame of government, are continued to us unimpaired, — demand of the whole American people sincere thanks to a benevolent Deity for the merciful dispensations of his providence."

1800. — Nov. 22. "A treaty of amity and commerce with the King of Prussia has been concluded and ratified. The envoys-extraordinary and ministers-plenipotentiary from the United States to France were received by the First Consul with the respect due to their character; and three persons with equal powers were appointed to treat with them.

"Immediately after the adjournment of Congress at their last session in Philadelphia, I gave directions, in compliance with the laws, for the removal of the public offices, records, and property. These directions have been executed; and the public officers have since resided, and conducted the ordinary business of the government, in this place (Washington). I congratulate the people of the United States on the assembling of Congress at the permanent seat of their government; and I congratulate you, gentlemen, on the prospect of a residence not to be changed.

"It would be unbecoming the representatives of this nation to assemble for the first time in this solemn temple without looking up to the Supreme Ruler of the universe, and imploring his blessing. May this territory be the residence of virtue and happiness! In this city may that piety and virtue, that wisdom and magnanimity, that constancy and self-government, which adorned the great character whose name it bears, be forever held in veneration! Here, and throughout our country, may simple manners, pure morals, and true religion, flourish forever! . . . "JOHN ADAMS."

JEFFERSON'S ADMINISTRATION.

1801 TO 1809.

THE CABINET.

· PRESIDENT:
THOMAS JEFFERSON, VIRGINIA.

VICE-PRESIDENTS:
1801. — AARON BURR, NEW YORK.
1805. — GEORGE CLINTON, NEW YORK.

SECRETARY OF STATE:
1801. — JAMES MADISON, Virginia.

SECRETARIES OF THE TREASURY:
1801. — S. DEXTER, Massachusetts.
1802. — ALBERT GALLATIN, Pennsylvania.

SECRETARY OF WAR:
1801. — HENRY DEARBORN, Massachusetts.

SECRETARIES OF THE NAVY:
1801. — BENJAMIN STODDERT, Maryland.
1802. — ROBERT SMITH, Maryland.
1805. — JACOB CROWNINSHIELD, Massachusetts.

POSTMASTERS-GENERAL:
1801. — JOSEPH HABERSHAM, Georgia.
1802. — GIDEON GRANGER, Connecticut.

ATTORNEYS-GENERAL:
1801. — THEOPHILUS PARSONS, Massachusetts (declined).
1801. — LEVI LINCOLN, Massachusetts.
1805. — ROBERT SMITH, Maryland.
1803. — JOHN BRECKENRIDGE, Kentucky.
1807. — CÆSAR A. RODNEY, Delaware.

CONTEMPORANEOUS ENGLISH HISTORY.

George III., King of England.
Mr. Addington, Prime-Minister, 1801 to 1804.
Mr. Pitt, Prime-Minister, 1804, until his death, at 47. in 1806.
Lord Grenville. and Duke of Portland, 1806 to 1809.
The Peace of Amiens in 1802.
Renewal of war with France in 1803.
Abolition of the slave-trade in 1807.
Peninsular War commenced in 1808.

THOMAS JEFFERSON.

FROM — 1801 to 1809.
DURATION. — Two terms, — eight years.
PARTY. — Republican (State-Sovereignty or Democratic).
PRINCIPAL EVENTS. — Ohio admitted into the Union in 1802. Louisiana ceded by Spain to France in 1800; purchased from France, for fifteen millions of dollars, in 1803. War with Tripoli, Africa, on account of seizures of American vessels. Duel between Burr and Hamilton, and death of the latter. Impressment of American seamen by British officers. Conspiracy of Burr to divide the Union: trial for treason; acquitted, 1807. American frigate "Chesapeake" fired into by the British frigate "Leopard." Embargo Act passed, December, 1807. Non-intercourse with Great Britain and France in 1809. James Madison elected President.

1801. — March 4. "About to enter, fellow-citizens, on the exercise of duties which comprehend every thing dear and valuable to you, it is proper you should understand what I deem the essential principles of our government, and, consequently, those which ought to shape its administration. I will compress them within the narrowest compass they will bear, stating the general principle, but not all its limitations: Equal and exact justice to all men, of whatever State or persuasion, religious or political; peace, commerce, and honest friendship, with all nations, entangling alliances with none; the support of the State governments in all their rights, as the most competent administrations for our domestic concerns, and the surest bulwarks against anti-republican tendencies; the preservation of the General Government in its whole constitutional vigor, as the sheet-anchor of our peace at home, and safety abroad; a jealous care of the right of election by the people, a mild and safe corrective of abuses which are lopped by the sword of revolution where peaceable remedies are unprovided; absolute acquiescence in the decisions of the majority, the vital principle of republics, from which there is no appeal but to force, the vital principle and immediate parent of despotism; a well-disciplined militia, our best reliance in peace, and for the first moments of war, till regulars may relieve them; the supremacy of the civil over the military authority; economy in the public expenses, that labor may be lightly burdened; the honest payment of our debts, and sacred preservation of the public faith; encouragement of agriculture, and of commerce as its handmaid; the diffusion of information, and arraignment of all abuses at the bar of the public reason; freedom of religion, freedom of the press, and freedom of person under the protection of the *habeas-corpus;* and trial by juries impartially selected. These principles form the bright constellation which has gone before us, and guided our steps through an age of revolution and reformation. The wisdom of our sages, and blood of our heroes, have been devoted to their attainment: they should be the creed of our political faith, the text of civic instruction, the touchstone by which to try the services of those we trust; and, should we wander from them in moments of error or of alarm, let us hasten to retrace our steps, and to regain the road which alone leads to peace, liberty, and safety. . . . I repair then, fellow-citizens, to the post you have assigned me, with experience enough in subordinate offices to have seen the difficulties of this, the greatest of all. I have learned to expect that it will rarely fall to the lot of imperfect man to retire from this station with the reputation and the favor which bring him into it. Without pretensions to that high confidence you reposed in our first and greatest revolutionary character, whose pre-eminent services entitled him to the first place in his country's love, and destined for him the fairest page in the volume of faithful history, I ask so much confidence only as may give firmness and effect to the legal administration of your affairs."

1801.—Dec. 8. "It is a circumstance of sincere gratification to me, that, on meeting the great council of the nation, I am able to announce to them, on grounds of reasonable certainty, that the wars and troubles which have for so many years afflicted our sister-nations have at length come to an end, and that the communications of peace and commerce are once more opening among them. Among our Indian neighbors, also, a spirit of peace and friendship generally prevails. We may now safely dispense with all the internal taxes, comprehending excises, stamps, auctions, licenses, carriages, and refined sugars. To this state of general peace with which we have been blessed one only exception exists. Tripoli, the least considerable of the Barbary States, has come forward with demands unfounded either in right or in compact, and has permitted itself to denounce war on our failure to comply before a given day. The style of the demand admitted but one answer. I sent a small squadron of frigates into the Mediterranean, with assurances to that power of our sincere desire to remain in peace, but with orders to protect our commerce against the threatened attack. The measure was seasonable and salutary. A statement has been formed by the secretary-at-war, on mature consideration, of all the posts and stations where garrisons will be expedient, and of the number of men requisite for each garrison. Uncertain as we must ever be of the particular point in our circumference where an enemy may choose to invade us, the only force which can be ready at every point, and competent to oppose them, is the body of neighboring citizens as formed into a militia. On these, collected from the parts most convenient in numbers proportioned to the invading force, it is best to rely, not only to meet the first attack, but, if it threatens to be permanent, to maintain the defence until regulars may be engaged to relieve them. Agriculture, manufactures, commerce, and navigation, the four pillars of our prosperity, are most thriving when left most free to individual enterprise. Protection from casual embarrassments, however, may sometimes be seasonably interposed. I cannot omit recommending a revisal of the laws on the subject of naturalization. Shall we refuse to the unhappy fugitives from distress that hospitality which the savages of the wilderness extended to our fathers arriving in this land? Shall oppressed humanity find no asylum on this globe? The Constitution, indeed, has wisely provided, that, for admission to certain offices of important trust, a residence shall be required sufficient to develop character and design; but might not the general character and capabilities of a citizen be safely communicated to every one manifesting a *bonâ-fide* purpose of embarking his life and fortunes permanently with us?"

1802.—Dec. 15. "Another year is come around, and finds us still blessed with peace and friendship abroad; law, order, and religion at home;

good affection and harmony with our Indian neighbors; our burdens lightened, yet our income sufficient for the public wants, and the produce of the year great beyond example. These, fellow-citizens, are the circumstances under which we meet; and we remark with special satisfaction those which, under the smiles of Providence, result from the skill, industry, and order of our citizens, managing their own affairs in their own way and for their own use, unembarrassed by too much regulation, unoppressed by fiscal exactions. In the department of finance, it is with pleasure I inform you that the receipts of external duties for the last twelve months have exceeded those of any former year, and that the ratio of increase has been also greater than usual. This has enabled us to answer all the regular exigencies of government; to pay from the treasury, within one year, upwards of eight millions of dollars, principal and interest, of the public debt, exclusive of upwards of one million paid by the sale of bank-stock, and making in the whole a reduction of nearly five millions and a half of principal; and to have now in the treasury four millions and a half of dollars, which are in a course of application to the further discharge of debt and current demands."

1803.—Oct. 17. "The property and sovereignty of all Louisiana has been transferred to the United States by instruments bearing date the 30th of April last. Should the acquisition be constitutionally confirmed and carried into effect, a sum of nearly thirteen millions of dollars will then be added to our public debt, most of which is payable after fifteen years; before which term the present existing debts will all be discharged by the established operation of the sinking-fund. We have seen with sincere concern the flames of war lighted up again in Europe, and nations with which we have the most friendly and useful relations engaged in mutual destruction. While we regret the miseries in which we see others involved, let us bow with gratitude to that kind Providence, which, inspiring with wisdom and moderation our late legislative councils while placed under the urgency of the greatest wrongs, guarded us from hastily entering into the sanguinary contest, and left us only to look on and to pity its ravages. These will be heaviest on those immediately engaged. Yet the nations pursuing peace will not be exempt from all evil. Separated by a wide ocean from the nations of Europe and from the political interests which entangle them together, with productions and wants which render our commerce and friendship useful to them, and theirs to us, it cannot be the interest of any to assail us, nor ours to disturb them. We should be most unwise indeed were we to cast away the singular blessings of the position in which Nature has placed us; the opportunity she has endowed us with of pursuing, at a distance from foreign contentions, the paths of industry, peace, and happiness, of cultivating general friendship, and of bringing collisions of interest to the umpire of reason rather than of force."

1804.—Nov. 8. Eighth Congress, second session. "With the nations of Europe in general our friendship and intercourse are undisturbed; and from the governments of the belligerent powers especially we continue to receive those friendly manifestations which are justly due to an honest neutrality, and to such good offices consistent with that as we have opportunities of rendering. The state of our finances continues to fulfil our expectation. Eleven millions and a half, received in the course of the last year ending on the 30th of September last, have enabled us, after meeting all the ordinary expenses of the year, to pay three million six hundred thousand dollars of the principal of the public debt. This payment, with those of the two preceding years, has extinguished upwards of twelve millions of the principal, and a greater sum of interest within that period."

1805. — March 4. Inaugural, second term. "The remaining revenue on the consumption of foreign articles is paid cheerfully by those who can afford to add foreign luxuries to domestic comforts. Being collected on our seaboard and frontiers only, and incorporated with the transactions of our mercantile citizens, it may be the pleasure and the pride of an American to ask, What farmer, what mechanic, what laborer, ever sees a tax-gatherer of the United States? I know that the acquisition of Louisiana has been disapproved by some from a candid apprehension that the enlargement of our territory would endanger its union. But who can limit the extent to which the federative principle may operate effectively? The larger our association, the less will it be shaken by local passions; and, in any view, is it not better that the opposite bank of the Mississippi should be settled by our own brethren and children than by strangers of another family? With which shall we be most likely to live in harmony and friendly intercourse? In matters of religion, I have considered that its free exercise is placed by the Constitution independent of the powers of the General Government. Contemplating the union of sentiment now manifested so generally as auguring harmony and happiness to our future course, I offer to our country sincere congratulations. With those, too, not yet rallied to the same point, the disposition to do so is gaining strength. Facts are piercing through the veil drawn over them; and our doubting brethren will at length see that the mass of their fellow-citizens, with whom they cannot yet resolve to act as to principles and measures, think as they think, and desire what they desire; that our wish, as well as theirs, is, that the public efforts may be directed honestly to the public good; that peace be cultivated, civil and religious liberty unassailed, law and order preserved, equality of rights maintained, and that state of property, equal or unequal, which results to every man from his own industry or that of his fathers. When satisfied of these views, it is not in human nature that they should not approve and support them. . . . I shall now enter on the duties to which my fellow-citizens have again called me. I shall need all the indulgence I have heretofore experienced: the want of it will certainly not lessen with increasing years. I shall need, too, the favor of that Being in whose hands we are; who led our forefathers, as Israel of old, from their native land, and planted them in a country flowing with all the necessaries and comforts of life; who has covered our infancy with his providence, and our riper years with his wisdom and power; and to whose goodness I ask you to join with me in supplications that he will so enlighten the minds of your servants, guide their counsels, and prosper their measures, that whatsoever they do shall result in your good, and shall secure to you the peace, friendship, and approbation of all nations."

1805.—Dec. 3. "Since our last meeting, the aspect of our foreign relations has considerably changed. Our coasts have been infested and our harbors watched by private-armed vessels; some of them without commissions, some with illegal commissions, others with those of legal form, but committing piratical acts beyond the authority of their commissions. They have captured in the very entrance of our harbors, as well as on the high seas, not only the vessels of our friends coming to trade with us, but our own also. They have carried them off under pretence of legal adjudication; but, not daring to approach a court of justice, they have plundered and sunk them by the way, or in obscure places, where no evidence could arise against them; maltreated the crews, and abandoned them in boats, in the open sea or on desert shores, without food or covering. These enormities appearing to be unreached by any control of their sovereigns, I found it necessary to equip a force to cruise within our own seas to arrest all vessels of these descriptions found hovering on our coasts within the limits of the Gulf Stream, and to bring the offenders in for trial as pirates. The same system of hovering on our coasts and harbors under color of seeking enemies has been also carried on by public-armed ships, to the great annoyance and oppression of our commerce. . . . With Spain our negotiations for a settlement of differences have not had a satisfactory issue. . . . On the Mobile, our commerce passing through that river continues to be obstructed by arbitrary duties and vexatious searches. Propositions for adjusting amicably the boundaries of Louisiana have not been acceded to. Inroads have been recently made into the territories of Orleans and the Mississippi. Our citizens have been seized and their property plundered in the very ports of the former, which had been actually delivered up by Spain, and this by the regular officers and soldiers of that government. . . . Turning from these unpleasant views of violence and wrong, I congratulate you on the liberation of our fellow-citizens who were stranded on the coast of Tripoli and made prisoners of war. In a government bottomed on the will of all, the life and liberty of every individual citizen becomes interesting to all. Congress, by their act of Nov. 10, 1803, authorized us to borrow one million seven hundred and fifty thousand dollars towards meeting the claims of our citizens assumed by the Convention with France. We have not, however, made use of this authority, because the sum of four millions and a half, which remained in the treasury on the same thirtieth day of September last, with the receipts which we may calculate on for the ensuing year, besides paying the annual sum of eight millions of dollars appropriated to the funded debt, and meeting all the current demands which may be expected, will enable us to pay the whole sum of three million seven hundred and fifty thousand dollars assumed by the French Convention, and still leave us a surplus of nearly a million of dollars at our free disposal."

1806.—Dec. 2. "The delays which have taken place in our negotiations with the British Government appear to have proceeded from causes which do not forbid the expectation, that, during the course of the session, I may be enabled to lay before you their final issue. What will be that of the negotiations for settling our differences with

Spain, nothing which had taken place at the date of the last despatches enables us to pronounce. On the western side of the Mississippi she advanced in considerable force, and took post at the settlement of Bayou Pierre, on the Red River. This village was originally settled by France, was held by her as long as she held Louisiana, and was delivered to Spain only as a part of Louisiana. . . . The possession of both banks of the Mississippi reducing to a single point the defence of that river, its waters, and the country adjacent, it becomes highly necessary to provide for that point a more adequate security. The gunboats authorized by an act of the last session are so advanced, that they will be ready for service in the ensuing spring. . . . The receipts at the treasury during the year ending on the thirtieth day of September last have amounted to near fifteen millions of dollars; which have enabled us, after meeting the current demands, to pay two million seven hundred thousand dollars of the American claims in part of the price of Louisiana; to pay of the funded debt upward of three millions of principal, and nearly four of interest; and, in addition, to re-imburse in the course of the present month near two millions of five and a half per cent stock. These payments and re-imbursements of the funded debt; with those which had been made in the four years and a half preceding, will, at the close of the present year, have extinguished upward of twenty-three millions of principal."

1807. — Oct. 27. "Circumstances, fellow-citizens, which seriously threatened the peace of our country, have made it a duty to convene you at an earlier period than usual. All the circumstances which induced the extraordinary mission to London are already known to you. . . . On the twenty-second day of June last, by a formal order from a British admiral, the frigate 'Chesapeake,' leaving her port for a distant service, was attacked by one of those vessels which had been lying in our harbors under the indulgences of hospitality; was disabled from proceeding; had several of her crew killed, and four taken away. On this outrage no commentaries are necessary. Its character has been pronounced by the indignant voice of our citizens with an emphasis and unanimity never exceeded. The aggression thus begun has been continued, on the part of the British commanders, by remaining within our waters in defiance of the authority of the country, by habitual violations of its jurisdiction, and at length by putting to death one of the persons whom they had forcibly taken from on board 'The Chesapeake.' To former violations of maritime rights, another is now added of very extensive effect. The government of that nation has issued an order interdicting all trade by neutrals between ports not in amity with them; and, being now at war with nearly every nation on the Atlantic and Mediterranean seas, our vessels are required to sacrifice their cargoes at the first port they touch, or to return without the benefit of going to any other market. Under this new law of the ocean, our trade on the Mediterranean has been swept away by seizures and condemnations; and that in other seas is threatened with the same fate. . . . Our differences with Spain remain still unsettled. . . . With the other nations of Europe our harmony has been uninterrupted. . . . The gunboats already provided have been chiefly assigned to New York, New Orleans, and the Chesapeake. . . . I informed

Congress, at their last session, of the enterprises against the public peace which were believed to be in preparation by Aaron Burr and his associates; of the measures taken to defeat them, and to bring the offenders to justice."

1808.—Nov. 8. "The communications made to Congress at their last session explained the posture in which the close of the discussion relative to the attack by a British ship of war on the frigate 'Chesapeake' left a subject on which the nation had manifested so honorable a sensibility. Every view of what had passed authorized a belief that immediate steps would be taken by the British Government for redressing a wrong, which, the more it was investigated, appeared the more clearly to require what had not been provided for in the special mission. It is found that no steps have been taken for the purpose. On the contrary, it will be seen in the documents laid before you that the inadmissible preliminary which obstructed the adjustment is still adhered to, and, moreover, that it is now brought into connection with the distinct and irrelative case of the orders in council. . . . With our Indian neighbors the public peace has been steadily maintained. . . . Of the gunboats authorized, it has been thought necessary to build only a hundred and three in the present year. . . . Considering the extraordinary character of the times in which we live, our attention should unremittingly be fixed on the safety of the country. For a people who are free, and who mean to remain so, a well organized and armed militia is their best security. . . . Availing myself of this, — the last occasion which will occur of addressing the two houses, — I cannot omit the expression of my sincere gratitude for the repeated proofs of confidence manifested to me by themselves and their predecessors since my call to the administration, and the many indulgences experienced at their hands. The same grateful acknowledgments are due to my fellow-citizens generally, whose support has been my great encouragement under all embarrassments. . . . Retiring from the charge of their affairs, I carry with me the consolation of a firm persuasion that Heaven has in store for our beloved country long ages to come of prosperity and happiness.

"**Thomas Jefferson.**"

MADISON'S ADMINISTRATION.

1809 TO 1817.

THE CABINET.

PRESIDENT:
JAMES MADISON, VIRGINIA.

VICE-PRESIDENTS:
GEORGE CLINTON, NEW YORK.
ELBRIDGE GERRY, MASSACHUSETTS.

SECRETARIES OF STATE:
1809.—ROBERT SMITH, Maryland.
1811.—JAMES MONROE, Virginia.

SECRETARIES OF THE TREASURY:
1809.—ALBERT GALLATIN, Pennsylvania.
1814.—G. W. CAMPBELL, Tennessee.
1814.—ALEXANDER J. DALLAS, Pennsylvania.

SECRETARIES OF WAR:
1809.—WILLIAM EUSTIS, Massachusetts.
1813.—JOHN ARMSTRONG, New York.
1814.—JAMES MONROE, Virginia.
1815.—WM. H. CRAWFORD, Georgia.

SECRETARIES OF THE NAVY:
1809.—PAUL HAMILTON, South Carolina.
1813.—WILLIAM JONES, Pennsylvania.
1814.—BENJAMIN W. CROWNINSHIELD, Massachusetts.

POSTMASTERS-GENERAL:
1809.—GIDEON GRANGER, Connecticut.
1814.—R. J. MEIGS, Ohio.

ATTORNEYS-GENERAL:
1809.—CÆSAR A. RODNEY, Delaware.
1811.—WILLIAM PINCKNEY, Maryland.
1814.—RICHARD RUSH, Pennsylvania.

CONTEMPORANEOUS ENGLISH HISTORY.

George III., King of England.
Mr. Spencer Perceval, Prime-Minister, 1810 to 1812. (Assassinated May 11.)
Lord Liverpool, Prime-Minister, 1812 to 1817.
Peninsular War, American War, and Waterloo.
Napoleon escapes from Elba, March 1, 1815. England, Austria, Prussia, and Russia allied against him. Returns to Paris the 20th; supplants Louis XVIII. Fights at Waterloo, June 18; abdicates on the 22d. Surrenders, and is exiled to St. Helena, July 15.
Vote of thanks and $1,000,000 presented to the Duke of Wellington.

JAMES MADISON.

FROM — 1809 to 1817.

DURATION. — Two terms, — eight years.

PARTY. — Republican.

PRINCIPAL EVENTS. — Continued difficulties with England. Favorable negotiations commenced with Erskine, the resident British minister. Intercourse again opened with Great Britain. Negotiations disavowed by the ministry. Non-intercourse re-established. Ocean covered with French and English cruisers, and Danish privateers, plundering American vessels. Bonaparte issues the "Rambouillet Decree" against American vessels entering French ports. One hundred and thirty-two ships captured and sold for eight million dollars by the French Government. Archangel, Russia, the only port open to the United States. Rencounter between the American frigate "President," off Delaware, and "The Little Belt." Inland troubles increase. In 1811, Tecumseh, and his twin-brother the Prophet, stir up a revolt. Gen. William Henry Harrison, the Governor of Indiana Territory, conquers at Tippecanoe. American commerce still interfered with. Impressment of American seamen. Henry Clay and John C. Calhoun members of the House. Question of peace, or war, agitated. Seaport towns against it; interior and Western towns for it. War declared June 18, 1812. Professorships established at West-Point Academy. Gen. Hull crosses from Detroit to Canada, and is forced to surrender to Gen. Brock, the governor. France repeals the Berlin and Milan Decrees, and Great Britain repeals her Orders in Council. Impressment question still unsettled. Six thousand cases on record at Washington. Sixteen hundred

Americans in British navy. British press-gangs led by insolent officers. Britain demands that Englishmen in America shall not enter our service, notwithstanding service is expected from Americans and others in England. Major-Gen. Dearborn and Gen. Van Rensselaer have charge of Lake Champlain; Capt. Chauncy, of the Lakes Erie and Ontario. Lieut. Elliot captures two vessels on Lake Erie. Lieut. Winfield Scott and Capt. Wool direct at Queenstown. Gen. Brock slain. "The Constitution," Old Ironsides, is chased by British ships four days, and escapes; is afterwards attacked by "The Guerrière" near the St. Lawrence, and captures her, Aug. 19, 1812. "The United States," Capt. Decatur, off the Azores, captures "The Macedonian." "The Wasp" captures "The Frolic." Both brigs afterward taken by "The Poictiers," seventy-four-gun ship. Near Brazil, "The Constitution" takes "The Java." Average loss in these engagements, eight of the English to one of the Americans. England is mortified at the loss of her frigates. America, flushed with victory, goes on to new conquests; and five hundred British vessels and three frigates are captured in seven months by the Americans. The West, aroused, forms three armies: Gen. Harrison, at Lake Erie; Gen. Dearborn, Ontario; Gen. Wade, Lake Champlain, against Gens. Prevost, Proctor, and Sheafe, in Canada. Gen. Winchester, advancing from Kentucky, is captured, and surrenders. Gen. Clay holds Fort Meigs against Tecumseh and Proctor. February, 1813.— Capt. James Lawrence of "The Hornet" captures "The Peacock" off South America; is promoted to the command of the frigate "Chesapeake," and falls mortally wounded in an engagement with "The Shannon" in Boston harbor. His last command was, "Don't give up the ship!" Lieut. Perry wins a victory at Lake Erie; his battle-flag being, "Don't give up the ship!" Col. Johnson, under Harrison, kills Tecumseh. Col. Lewis Cass garrisons Detroit. Gen. Andrew Jackson defends New Orleans. Commodore Chauncy and Lieut. Scott attack Toronto, and obtain the control of Lake Ontario. Gen. McClure indiscreetly destroys Fort George, and fires the village of Newark; and, December, 1813, Gen. Prevost retaliates, and burns every house reached on both Lakes. June, 1813. — The entire American coast is blockaded by British ships; and Tennessee and Georgia are disturbed by the Creeks, Cherokees, and Choctaws. Forsyth of Georgia, Gaston of North Carolina, McLean of Ohio, and Daniel Webster, are elected to Congress. New England opposes the war. The Massachusetts Legislature remonstrates against it. July, 1814. — A midnight battle is fought at Lundy's Lane, and Col. Winfield Scott is wounded. Sept. 11 occurred the battle of Lake Champlain. The British fleet enters Chesapeake Bay. Washington, Baltimore, and Annapolis are threatened. Gen. Ross moves to Bladensburg, where a memorable battle is fought, and from thence to Washington: and the Capitol, Congressional Library, and other public buildings, are destroyed by fire. Gen. Ross is killed on the Chesapeake, near Baltimore. The song of the "Star-spangled Banner" was composed by Francis Key during the attack on Fort McHenry. Marauding expeditions line the coast from Eastport to Sandy Hook. Hartford Convention, Dec. 15, 1814. Gen. Jackson seizes Pensacola, and wins the battle of New Orleans, Jan. 8, 1815. Meanwhile the peace signed at Ghent, December, 1814, is on the way from Europe. Unbounded excitement and joy throughout the land. A day of thanksgiving observed. War debt, $100,000,000. National Bank organized, with a capital of $35,000,000; charter, twenty years. Currency redeemable with gold and silver. Algerine War. Robert Fulton propels a boat by steam. James Monroe elected President.

1809. — March 4. "Indulging no passions which trespass on the rights or repose of other nations, it has been the true glory of the United States to cultivate peace by observing justice, and to entitle themselves to the respect of the nations at war by fulfilling their neutral obligations with the most scrupulous impartiality. If there be candor in the world, the truth of these assertions will not be questioned. Posterity, at least, will do justice to them. This unexceptionable course could not avail against the injustice and violence of the belligerent powers. In their rage against each other, or impelled by more direct motives, principles of retaliation have been introduced, equally contrary to universal reason and acknowledged law. How long their arbitrary edicts will be continued in spite of the demonstration that not even a pretext for them has been given by the United States, and of the fair and liberal attempts to induce a revocation of them, cannot be anticipated. Assuring myself, that, under every vicissitude, the determined spirit and united counsels of the nation will be safeguards to its honor and its essential interests, I repair to the post assigned me, with no other discouragement than what springs from my own inadequacy to its high duties. . . . It is my good fortune to have the path in which I am to tread lighted by examples of illustrious services successfully rendered in the most trying difficulties by those who have marched before me. But the source to which I look for the aid which alone can supply my deficiencies is in the well-tried intelligence and virtue of my fellow-citizens, and in the counsels of those representing them in the other departments associated in the care of the national interests. In these my confidence will, under every difficulty, be best placed, next to that we have all been encouraged to feel in the guardianship and guidance of that Almighty Being whose power regulates the destiny of nations, whose blessings have been so conspicuously dispensed to this rising republic, and to whom we are bound to address our devout gratitude for the past, as well as our fervent supplications and best hopes for the future."

1809.—May 23. To both houses of Congress: "On this first occasion of meeting you, it affords me much satisfaction to be able to communicate the commencement of a favorable change in our foreign relations, the critical state of which induced a session of Congress at this early period. The revision of our commercial laws, proper to adapt them to the arrangement which has taken place with Great Britain, will doubtless engage the early attention of Congress. Under the existing aspect of affairs, I have thought it not inconsistent with a just precaution to have the gun-boats, with the exception of those at New Orleans, placed in a situation incurring no expense beyond that requisite for their preservation, and convenience for future service. . . . I have thought, also, that our citizens, detached in quotas of militia, might not improperly be relieved from the State in which they are held for immediate service. A discharge of them has accordingly been directed."

1809.—Nov. 29. "At the period of our last meeting, I had the satisfaction of communicating an adjustment with one of the principal belligerent nations, highly important in itself, and still more so as presaging a more extended accommodation. It is with deep concern I am now to inform you that the favorable prospect has been overclouded by a refusal of the British Government to abide by the act of its minister-plenipotentiary, and by its ensuing policy towards the United States.

"With France, the other belligerent, whose trespasses on our commercial rights have long been the subject of our just remonstrances, the posture of our relations does not correspond with the measures taken on the part of the United States to effect a favorable change. In relation to the powers on the coast of Barbary, nothing has occurred which is not of a nature rather to inspire confidence than distrust as to the continuance of the existing amity. With our Indian neighbors, the just and benevolent system continued towards them has also preserved peace, and is more and more advancing habits favorable to their civilization and happiness.

"The fortifications on our maritime frontiers are in many of the ports completed. By the enlargement of the works, and the employment of a great number of hands at the public armories, the supply of small arms appears to be annually increasing at a rate that may be expected to go far towards providing for the public exigency. The sums which had been previously accumulated in the treasury, together with the receipts during the year ending Sept. 30 (amounting to more than nine millions of dollars), have enabled us to fulfil all our engagements, and to defray the current expenses of government, without recurring to any loan. In the state which has been presented of our affairs with the great parties of a disastrous war, carried on in a mode equally injurious and unjust to the United States as a neutral nation, the wisdom of the National Legislature will be again summoned to the important decision on the alternatives before them. That these will be met in a spirit worthy the counsels of a nation conscious both of its rectitude and of its rights, and careful as well of its honor as of its peace, I have an entire confidence.

"In the midst of the wrongs and vexations experienced from external causes, there is much room for congratulation on the prosperity and happiness flowing from our situation at home. The blessing of health has never been more universal. . . . Nor is it unworthy of reflection, that this revolution in our pursuits and habits is in no slight degree a consequence of those impolitic and arbitrary edicts by which the contending nations, in endeavoring, each of them, to abstract our trade with the other, have so far abridged our means of procuring the productions and manufactures of which our own are now taking the place. Recollecting always, that, for every advantage which may contribute to distinguish our lot from that to which others are doomed by the unhappy spirit of the times, we are indebted to that Divine Providence whose goodness has been so remarkably extended to this rising nation, it becomes us to cherish a devout gratitude, and to implore from the same omnipotent source a blessing on the consultations and measures about to be undertaken for the welfare of our beloved country."

1810. — Dec. 5. "Among the commercial abuses still committed under the American flag, and leaving in force my former reference to that subject, it appears that American citizens are instrumental in carrying on a traffic in enslaved Africans, equally in violation of the laws of humanity, and in defiance of those of their own country. The same just and benevolent motives which produced the interdiction in force against this criminal conduct will doubtless be felt by Congress in devising further means of suppressing the evil.

"The receipts into the treasury during the year ending Sept. 30 last (and amounting to more than eight million and a half of dollars) have exceeded the current expenses of the government, including the interest on the public debt."

1811. — Nov. 5. "In calling you together sooner than a separation from your home would otherwise have required, I yielded to considerations drawn from the posture of our foreign affairs. Indemnity and redress for wrongs have continued to be withheld; and our coasts, and the mouths of our harbors, have again witnessed scenes not less derogatory to the dearest of our national rights than vexatious to the regular course of our trade. Among the occurrences produced by the conduct of British ships of war hovering on our coasts was an encounter between one of them and the American frigate commanded by Capt. Rodgers, rendered unavoidable on the part of the latter, by a fire, commenced without cause, by the former; whose commander is, therefore, alone chargeable with the blood unfortunately shed in maintaining the honor of the American flag. . . . In addition, the United States have much reason to be dissatisfied with the rigorous and unexpected restrictions to which their trade with the French dominions has been subjected, and which, if not discontinued, will require at least corresponding restrictions on importations from France into the United States. . . . Our other foreign relations remain without unfavorable changes. With Russia they are on the best footing of friendship. The ports of Sweden have afforded proofs of friendly disposition towards our commerce in the counsels of that nation also; and the information from our special minister to Denmark shows that the mission has been attended with valuable effects to our citizens, whose property had been so extensively violated and endangered by cruisers under the Danish flag.

"The receipts into the treasury, during the year ending Sept. 30 last, have exceeded thirteen millions and a half of dollars, and have enabled us to defray the current expenses, including the interest on the public debt, and to re-imburse more than five millions of dollars of the principal without recurring to the loan authorized by the act of the last session."

1812.—Nov. 4. "On our present meeting, it is my first duty to invite your attention to the providential favors which our country has experienced in the unusual degree of health dispensed to its inhabitants, and in the rich abundance with which the earth has rewarded the labors bestowed upon it. In the successful cultivation of other branches of industry, and in the progress of general improvement favorable to the national prosperity, there is just occasion, also, for our mutual congratulations and thankfulness. With these blessings are necessarily mingled the pressures and vicissitudes incident to the state of war into which the United States have been forced by the perseverance of a foreign power in its system of injustice and aggression. . . . Our expectation of gaining the command of the Lakes by the invasion of Canada from Detroit having been disappointed, measures were instantly taken to provide for them a naval force superior to that of the enemy. . . . On the coasts and on the ocean, the war has been as successful as circumstances inseparable from its early stages could promise. In the instances in which skill and bravery were more particularly tried, the American flag had an auspicious triumph. Anxious to abridge the evils from which a state of war cannot be exempt, I lost no time, after it was declared, in conveying to the British Government the terms on which its progress might be arrested. The advance was declined, from an avowed repugnance to a suspension of the practice of impressment during the armistice, and without any intimation that the arrangement proposed with respect to seamen would be accepted. The Indian tribes not under foreign instigations remain at peace, and receive the civilizing attentions which have proved so beneficial to them."

1813.— March 4. Extracts from Inaugural Address : "The war with a powerful nation, which forms so prominent a feature in our situation, is stamped with that justice which invites the smiles of Heaven on the means of conducting it to a successful termination. It was not declared on the part of the United States until it had been long made on them in reality, though not in name; until arguments and expostulations had been exhausted; until a positive declaration had been received, that the wrongs provoking it would not be discontinued; nor until this appeal could no longer be delayed without breaking down the spirit of the nation, destroying all confidence in itself and in its political institutions, and either perpetuating a state of disgraceful suffering, or regaining by more costly sacrifices and more severe struggles our lost rank and respect among independent powers. On the issue of the war are staked our national sovereignty on the high seas, and the security of an important class of citizens, whose occupations give the proper value to those of every other class. I need not call into view the unlawfulness of the practice by which our mariners are forced, at the will of every cruising officer, from their own vessels into foreign ones, nor paint the outrages inseparable from it. The proofs are in the records of each successive administration of our government, and the cruel sufferings of that portion of the American people have found their way to every bosom not dead to the sympathies of human nature. As the war was just in its origin, and necessary and noble in its objects, we can reflect with a proud satisfaction, that, in carrying it on, no principle of justice or honor, no usage of civilized nations, no precept of courtesy or humanity, has been infringed. How little has been the effect of this example on the conduct of the enemy! They have retained as prisoners of war citizens of the United States not liable to be so considered under the usages of war. They have refused to consider as prisoners of war, and threatened to punish as traitors and deserters, persons emigrating without restraint to the United States, incorporated by naturalization into our political family, and fighting under the authority of their adopted country in open and honorable war for the maintenance of its rights and safety. Such is the avowed purpose of a government which is in the practice of naturalizing by thousands citizens of other countries, and not only of permitting, but compelling, them to fight its battles against their native country. They have not, it is true, taken into their own hands the hatchet and the knife, devoted to indiscriminate massacre; but they have let loose the savages armed with these cruel instruments, have allured them into their service, and carried them to battle by their sides, eager to glut their savage thirst with the blood of the vanquished, and to finish the work of torture and death on maimed and defenceless captives. And, what was never before seen, British commanders have extorted victory over the unconquerable valor of our troops by presenting, to the sympathy of their chief, captives awaiting massacre from their savage associates; and now we find them, in further contempt of the modes of honorable warfare, supplying the place of a conquering force by attempts to disorganize our political society, to dismember our confederate republic."

1813.—Dec. 7. "In meeting you at the present interesting conjuncture, it would have been highly satisfactory if I could have communicated a favorable result to the mission charged with negotiations for restoring peace. The British cabinet, either mistaking our desire of peace for a dread of British power, or misled by other fallacious calculations, has disappointed this reasonable anticipation. The mediation was declined on the first instance; and there is no evidence, notwithstanding the lapse of time, that a change of disposition in the British counsels has taken place, or is to be expected. Under such circumstances, a nation proud of its rights, and conscious of its strength, has no choice but an exertion of the one in support of the other. To this determination, the best encouragement is derived from the success with which it has pleased the Almighty to bless our arms both on the land and on the water. The views of the French Government on the subjects which have been so long committed to negotiation have received no elucidation since the close of your last session. The war, with all its vicissitudes, is illustrating the capacity and the destiny of the United States to be a great, a flourishing, and a powerful nation, worthy of the friendship which it is disposed to cultivate with all others, and authorized by its own example to require from all an observance of the laws of justice and reciprocity. Beyond these their claims have never extended; and, in contending for these, we behold a subject for our congratulations in the daily testimonies of increasing harmony throughout the nation, and may humbly repose our trust in the smiles of Heaven on so righteous a course."

1814. — Sept. 20. "It is not to be disguised that the situation of our country calls for its greatest efforts. Our enemy is powerful in men and money, on the land and on the water. Availing himself of fortuitous advantages, he is aiming with his undivided force a deadly blow at our growing prosperity, — perhaps at our national existence. He has avowed his purpose of trampling on the usages of civilized warfare, and given earnests of it in the plunder and wanton destruction of private property. In his pride of maritime dominion, and in his thirst of commercial monopoly, he strikes with peculiar animosity at the progress of our navigation and our manufactures. His barbarous policy has not even spared those monuments of the arts and models of taste with which our country had enriched and embellished its infant metropolis. From such an adversary, hostility in its greatest force and in its worst forms may be looked for. The American people will face it with the undaunted spirit, which, in their Revolutionary struggle, defeated his unrighteous projects. His threats and his barbarities, instead of dismay, will kindle in every bosom an indignation not to be extinguished but in the disaster and expulsion of such cruel invaders. In providing the means necessary, the National Legislature will not distrust the heroic and enlightened patriotism of its constituents. They will cheerfully and proudly bear every burden of every kind which the safety and honor of the nation demand. We have seen them everywhere paying their taxes, direct and indirect, with the greatest promptness and alacrity. We see them rushing with enthusiasm to the scenes where danger and duty call. In offering their blood, they give the surest pledge that no other tribute will be withheld. Having forborne to declare war until to other aggressions had been added the capture of nearly a thousand American vessels and the impressment of thousands of American seafaring citizens, and until a final declaration had been made by the government of Great Britain that her hostile orders against our commerce would not be revoked but on conditions as impossible as unjust, whilst it was known that these orders would not otherwise cease but with a war which had lasted nearly twenty years, and which, according to appearances at that time, might last as many more; having manifested on every occasion, and in every proper mode, a sincere desire to arrest the effusion of blood, and meet our enemy on the ground of justice and reconciliation, — our beloved country, in still opposing to his persevering hostility all its energies with an undiminished disposition toward peace and friendship on honorable terms, must carry with it the good wishes of the impartial world, and the best hopes of support from an omnipotent and kind Providence.".

1815.—Feb. 18. Five months later, the President addresses Congress as follows: "I lay before Congress copies of the treaty of peace and amity between the United States and his Britannic Majesty which was signed by the commissioners of both parties at Ghent on the 24th December, 1814, and the ratifications of which have been duly exchanged. While performing this act, I congratulate you and our constituents upon an event which is highly honorable to the nation, and terminates with peculiar felicity a campaign signalized by the most brilliant successes. Peace, at all times a blessing, is peculiarly welcome at a period when the causes for the war have ceased to operate; when the government has demonstrated the efficiency of its powers of defence; and when the nation can review its conduct without regret and without reproach. *I recommend to your care and beneficence the gallant men whose achievements in every department of the military service, on the land and on the water, have so essentially contributed to the honor of the American name and to the restoration of peace. The feelings of conscious patriotism and worth will animate such men under every change of fortune and pursuit; but their country performs a duty to itself when it bestows those testimonials of approbation and applause which are at once the reward of and the incentive to great actions.* . . . The termination of the legislative sessions will soon separate you, fellow-citizens, from each other, and restore you to your constituents. I pray you to bear with you the expressions of my sanguine hope, that the peace which has been just declared will not only be the foundation of the most friendly intercourse between the United States and Great Britain, but that it will also be productive of happiness and harmony in every section of our beloved country. The influence of your precepts and example must be everywhere powerful; and, while we accord in grateful acknowledgments for the protection which Providence has bestowed upon us, let us never cease to inculcate obedience to the laws, and fidelity to the Union, as constituting the palladium of the national independence and prosperity."

1815.—Dec. 5. "I have the satisfaction, on our present meeting, of being able to communicate to you the successful termination of the war which had been commenced against the United States by the regency of Algiers. It is another source of satisfaction that the treaty with Great Britain has been succeeded by a convention on the subject of commerce, concluded by the plenipotentiaries of the two countries. The national debt, as it was ascertained on the 1st of October last, amounted in the whole to the sum of a hundred and twenty millions of dollars, consisting of the unredeemed balance of the debt contracted before the late war (thirty-nine millions of dollars), the amount of the funded debt contracted in consequence of the war (sixty-four millions of dollars), and the amount of the unfunded and floating debt (including the various issues of treasury-notes), seventeen millions of dollars, which is in a gradual course of payment. The improved condition of the public revenue will not only afford the means of maintaining the faith of the government with its creditors inviolate, and of prosecuting successfully the measures of the most liberal policy, but will also justify an immediate alleviation of the burdens imposed by the necessities of war. Among the means of advancing the public interest, the occasion is a proper one for recalling the attention of Congress to the great importance of establishing throughout our country the roads and canals which can best be executed under the national authority. No objects within the circle of political economy so richly repay the expense bestowed on them. The present is a favorable season, also, for bringing into view the establishment of a national seminary of learning within the District of Columbia.

"In closing this communication, I ought not to repress a sensibility, in which you will unite, to the happy lot of our country, and the goodness of a superintending Providence to which we are indebted for it. Whilst other portions of mankind are laboring under the distresses of war, or struggling with adversity in other forms, the United States are in the tranquil enjoyment of prosperous and honorable peace. In reviewing the scenes through which it has been attained, we can rejoice in the proofs given that our political institutions — founded in human rights, and framed for their preservation — are equal to the severest trials of war, as well as adapted to the ordinary periods of repose. As fruits of this experience, and of the reputation acquired by the American arms on the land and on the water, the nation finds itself possessed of a growing respect abroad, and of a just confidence in itself, which are among the best pledges for its peaceful career. Under other aspects of our country, the strongest features of its flourishing condition are seen in a population rapidly increasing on a territory as productive as it is extensive; in a general industry and fertile ingenuity, which find their ample rewards; and in an affluent revenue, which admits a reduction of the public burdens without withdrawing the means of sustaining the public credit, of gradually discharging the public debt, of providing for the necessary defensive and precautionary establishments, and of patronizing, in every authorized mode, undertakings conducive to the aggregate wealth and individual comfort of our citizens."

1816.— Dec. 3. "Amidst the advantages which have succeeded the peace of Europe and that of the United States with Great Britain, in a general invigoration of industry among us, and in the extension of commerce; it is to be regretted that a depression is experienced by particular branches of our manufactures, and by a portion of our navigation. As the first proceeds, in an essential degree, from an excess of imported merchandise, which carries a check in its own tendency, the cause, in its present extent, cannot be of very long duration. The evil will not, however, be viewed by Congress without a recollection that manufacturing establishments, if suffered to sink too low or languish too long, may not revive after the causes shall have ceased; and that, in the vicissitudes of human affairs, situations may recur in which a dependence on foreign sources for indispensable supplies may be among the most serious embarrassments. The depressed state of our navigation is to be ascribed in a material degree to its exclusion from the colonial ports of the nation most extensively connected with us in commerce, and from the indirect operation of that exclusion. . . . I have the satisfaction to state, generally, that we remain in amity with foreign powers. An occurrence has indeed taken place in the Gulf of Mexico, which, if sanctioned by the Spanish Government, may make an exception as to that power. The posture of our affairs with Algiers at the present moment is not known: with the other Barbary States our affairs have undergone no change. The Indian tribes within our limits appear also to remain at peace. . . . Congress will call to mind that no adequate provision has yet been made for the uniformity of weights and measures also contemplated by the Constitution. The great utility of a standard fixed in its nature, and founded on the easy rule of decimal proportions, is sufficiently obvious. It led the government at an early stage to preparatory steps for introducing it; and a completion of the work will be a just title to the public gratitude. . . . The United States having been the first to abolish, within the extent of their authority, the transportation of the natives of Africa into slavery, by prohibiting the introduction of slaves, and by punishing their citizens participating in the traffic, cannot but be gratified at the progress made by concurrent efforts of other nations towards a general suppression of so great an evil. . . . In directing the legislative attention to the state of the finances, it is a subject of great gratification to find, that, even within the short period which has elapsed since the return of peace, the revenue has far exceeded all the current demands upon the treasury; and that, under any probable diminution of its future annual products which the vicissitudes of commerce may occasion, it will afford an ample fund for the effectual and early extinguishment of the public debt. The aggregate of the funded debt, composed of debts incurred during the wars of 1776 and 1812, has been estimated, with reference to January next, at a sum not exceeding a hundred and ten millions of dollars. The Bank of the United States has been organized under auspices the most favorable, and cannot fail to be an important auxiliary in financial matters. . . . The period of my retiring from the public service being at a little distance, I shall find no occasion more proper than the present for expressing to my fellow-citizens my deep sense of the continued confidence and kind support which I have received from them. My grateful recollections of these distinguished marks of their favorable regard can never cease, and, with the consciousness, that, if I have not served my country with great ability, I have served it with a sincere devotion, will accompany me as a source of unfailing gratification. . . . I can indulge the proud reflection, that the American people have reached in safety and success the fortieth year as an independent nation. . . . Nor is it less a peculiar felicity of this Constitution, so dear to us all, that it is found to be capable, without losing its vital energies, of expanding itself over a spacious territory, with the increase and expansion of the community for whose benefit it was established. "JAMES MADISON."

MONROE'S ADMINISTRATION.

1817 TO 1825.

THE CABINET.

PRESIDENT:
JAMES MONROE, Virginia.

VICE-PRESIDENT:
DANIEL D. TOMPKINS, New York.

SECRETARY OF STATE:
1817.—John Quincy Adams, Massachusetts.

SECRETARY OF THE TREASURY:
1817.—William H. Crawford, Georgia.

SECRETARIES OF WAR:
1817.—Isaac Shelby, Kentucky (declined).
1817.—John C. Calhoun, South Carolina.

SECRETARIES OF THE NAVY:
1817.—Benjamin W. Crowninshield, Massachusetts.
1818.—Smith Thompson, New York.
1823.—Samuel L. Southard, New Jersey.

POSTMASTERS-GENERAL:
1817.—R. J. Meigs, Ohio.
1823.—John McLean, Ohio.

ATTORNEY-GENERAL:
1817.—William Wirt, Virginia.

CONTEMPORANEOUS ENGLISH HISTORY.

George III. (Regency) and George IV.
Lord Liverpool, Prime-Minister, 1812 to 1827.
Suspension of the Habeas-Corpus Act in February and June, 1817, and August, 1822.
Death of George III., January, 1820.
Great prosperity in 1823 and 1824.
Monetary crisis in 1825.

JAMES MONROE.

FROM — March 4, 1817, to 1825.
DURATION. — Two terms, — eight years.
PARTY. — Republican (State-rights).
PRINCIPAL EVENTS. — Eastern States visited by the President: "Federal Boston" calls him a Federalist. Party differences gradually subsiding. Washington's revenue and foreign policy generally adopted. Colonization Society organized: Henry Clay and John Randolph vote for it. Seminole War, 1817. Gen. Jackson marches into Florida, and Pensacola is taken. Treaty with Spain, and cession of Florida to the United States, in 1821. for five million dollars and our claims to Texas. Financial embarrassments. Webster favors free trade. ("Let us not suppose that we are beginning the protection of manufactures by duties on imports. . . . Suppose all nations to act upon this principle, they would be prosperous, then, according to the argument, precisely in the proportion in which they abolished intercourse with one another.") Henry Clay favors protection. A protective tariff is passed, and manufacturers are greatly encouraged. Country agitated for two years, 1820 and 1821, on the slavery question. Union threatened. Fourteen thousand slaves smuggled into the United States from Africa and the West Indies. The *Monroe Doctrine* advanced Dec. 2, 1823 (see Message). Mississippi, Illinois, Alabama, Maine, and Missouri added to the Union, — the latter in August, 1821, under the Missouri Compromise; slavery to be excluded from all territory west of the Mississippi, north

of 36° 30'. Gen. Lafayette revisits the United States in 1824, and returns to France in 1825. Whole administration designated the "*era of good feeling.*" John Quincy Adams elected President.

1817.—March 4. "It is particularly gratifying to me to enter on the discharge of my duties at a time when the United States are blessed with peace. It is a state most consistent with their prosperity and happiness. It will be my sincere desire to preserve it, so far as depends on the Executive, on just principles, with all nations; claiming nothing unreasonable of any, and rendering to each what is its due. Equally gratifying is it to witness the increased harmony of opinion which pervades our Union. Discord does not belong to our system. Union is recommended as well by the free and benign principles of our government, extending its blessings to every individual, as by the other eminent advantages attending it. The American people have encountered together great dangers, and sustained severe trials with success. They constitute one great family with a common interest. Experience has enlightened us on some questions of essential importance to the country. . . . Never did a government commence under auspices so favorable, nor ever was success so complete. If we look to the history of other nations, ancient and modern, we find no example of a growth so rapid, so gigantic, of a people so prosperous and happy. In contemplating what we have still to perform, the heart of every citizen must expand with joy when he reflects how near our government has approached to perfection; that, in respect to it, we have no essential improvement to make; that the great object is to preserve it in the essential principles and features which characterize it; and that it is to be done by preserving the virtue and enlightening the minds of the people; and, as a security against foreign dangers, to adopt such arrangements as are indispensable to the support of our independence, our rights and liberties. If we persevere in the career in which we have advanced so far, and in the path already traced, we cannot fail, by the favor of a gracious Providence, to attain the high destiny which seems to await us. In the administrations of the illustrious men who have preceded me in this high station, with some of whom I have been connected by the closest ties from early life" (four of the first five presidents of the United States — Washington, Jefferson, Madison, and Monroe — were from Virginia), "examples are presented which will always be found highly instructive and useful to their successors. From these I shall endeavor to derive all the advantages which they may afford. . . . Relying on the aid to be derived from the other departments of the government, I enter on the trust to which I have been called by the suffrages of my fellow-citizens, with my fervent prayers to the Almighty that he will be graciously pleased to continue to us that protection which he has already so conspicuously displayed in our favor."

1817. — Dec. 2. "In contemplating the happy situation of the United States, our attention is drawn, with peculiar interest, to the surviving officers and soldiers of our Revolutionary army, who so eminently contributed by their services to lay its foundation. Most of those very meritorious citizens have paid the debt of nature, and gone to repose. It is believed, that, among the survivors, there are some, not provided for by existing laws, who are reduced to indigence, and even to real distress. These men have a claim on the gratitude of their country, and it will do honor to their country to provide for them. The lapse of a few years more, and the opportunity will be forever lost. . . . Respecting taxes, I consider it my duty to recommend to Congress their repeal. To impose taxes when the public exigencies require them is an obligation of the most sacred character, especially with a free people. The faithful fulfilment of it is among the highest proofs of their virtue, and capacity for self-government. To dispense with taxes, when it may be done with perfect safety, is equally the duty of their representatives."

1818.—Nov. 17. "In authorizing Major-Gen. Jackson to enter Florida in pursuit of the Seminoles, care was taken not to encroach on the rights of Spain. I regret to have to add, that, in executing this order, facts were disclosed respecting the conduct of the officers of Spain in authority there, in encouraging the war, furnishing munitions of war, and other supplies to carry it on, and in other acts not less marked, which evinced their participation in the hostile purposes of that combination, and justified the confidence with which it inspired the savages, that by those officers they would be protected. . . . The civil war which has so long prevailed between Spain and the provinces in South America still continues, without any prospect of its speedy termination. . . . Our relations with France, Russia, and other powers, continue on the most friendly basis."

1819. — Dec. 7. "Although the pecuniary embarrassments which affected various parts of the Union during the latter part of the preceding year, have, during the present, been considerably augmented, and still continue to exist, the receipts into the treasury, to the 30th of September last, have amounted to nineteen millions of dollars. After defraying the current expenses of the government, including the interest and re-imbursement of the public debt payable to that period, amounting to eighteen million two hundred thousand dollars, there remained in the treasury on that day more than two million five hundred thousand dollars, which, with the sums receivable during the remainder of the year, will exceed the current demands upon the treasury for the same period."

1820.—Nov. 14. "On the 30th of September, 1815, the funded and floating debt of the United States was estimated at a hundred and nineteen millions six hundred and thirty-five thousand dollars. If to this sum be added the amount of five per cent stock subscribed to the Bank of the United States, the amount of the Mississippi stock, and of the stock which was issued subsequently to that date, the balances ascertained to be due to certain States for military services, and to individuals for supplies furnished and services rendered during the late war, the public debt may be estimated as amounting at that date, and as afterwards liquidated, to a hundred and fifty-eight millions seven hundred and thirteen thousand dollars. On the 30th September, 1820, it amounted to ninety-one millions nine hundred and ninety-three thousand dollars; having been reduced in that interval, by payments, sixty-six millions of dollars. . . . The direct tax and excise were repealed soon after the termination of the late war; and the revenue has been derived almost wholly from other sources."

1821.—March 4. "It is now rather more than forty-four years since we declared our independence, and thirty-seven since it was acknowledged. The talents and virtues which were displayed in that great struggle were a sure presage of all that has since followed. A people who were able to surmount in their infant state such great perils, would be more competent, as they rose into manhood, to repel any which they might meet in their progress. . . . In this great nation there is but one order, that of the people, whose power, by a peculiarly happy improvement of the representative principle, is transferred from them without impairing in the slightest degree their sovereignty to bodies of their own creation, and to persons elected by themselves, in the full extent necessary, for all the purposes of free, enlightened, and efficient government. The whole system is elective, the complete sovereignty being in the people, and every officer, in every department, deriving his authority from and being responsible to them for his conduct. . . . With full confidence in the continuance of that candor and generous indulgence from my fellow-citizens at large which I have heretofore experienced, and with a firm reliance on the protection of Almighty God, I shall forthwith commence the duties of the high trust to which you have again called me."

1821.—Dec. 3. "With Spain, the treaty of Feb. 22, 1819, has been partly carried into execution. . . . Possession of East and West Florida has been given to the United States. Both provinces were formed into one territory, and a governor appointed for it. Two secretaries were appointed; the one to reside at Pensacola, and the other at St. Augustine."

1822.—Dec. 3. "The United States owe to the world a great example, and, by means thereof, to the cause of liberty and humanity a generous support. They have so far succeeded to the satisfaction of the virtuous and enlightened of every country. There is no reason to doubt that their whole movement will be regulated by a sacred regard to principle; all our institutions being founded on that basis. It has been often charged against free governments, that they have neither the foresight nor the virtue to provide at the proper season for great emergencies; that their course is improvident and expensive; that war will always find them unprepared; and, whatever may be its calamities, that its terrible warnings will be disregarded and forgotten as soon as peace returns. I have full confidence that this charge, so far as relates to the United States, will be shown to be utterly destitute of truth."

1823. — Dec. 2. "It appearing, from long experience, that no satisfactory arrangement could be formed of the commercial intercourse between the United States and the British Colonies in this hemisphere, by legislative acts, while each party pursued its own course, without agreement or concert with the other, a proposal has been made to the British Government to regulate this commerce by treaty. . . .

"The usual orders have been given to all our public ships to seize American vessels engaged in the slave-trade, and bring them in for adjudication; and I have the gratification to state, that not one so employed has been discovered; and there is good reason to believe that our flag is now seldom, if at all, disgraced by that traffic. . . . The sum which was appropriated at the last session for the repairs of the Cumberland Road has been applied with good effect to that object. . . . Many patriotic and enlightened citizens have suggested an improvement of still greater importance. They are of opinion the waters of the Chesapeake and Ohio may be connected together by one continued canal. . . . Connecting the Atlantic with the Western country in a line passing through the seat of the National Government, it would contribute essentially to strengthen the bond of union itself. Believing, as I do, that Congress possess the right to appropriate money for such a national object (the jurisdiction remaining to the States through which the canal would pass), I submit it to your consideration, whether it may not be advisable to authorize, by an adequate appropriation, the employment of a suitable number of the officers of the corps of engineers to examine the unexplored ground during the next session, and to report their opinion thereon. It will likewise be proper to extend their examination to the several routes through which the waters of the Ohio may be connected by canals with those of Lake Erie. . . . The citizens of the United States cherish sentiments the most friendly in favor of the liberty and happiness of their fellow-men on the other side of the Atlantic. In the wars of the European powers in matters relating to themselves we have never taken any part, nor does it comport with our policy to do so. It is only when our rights are invaded, or seriously menaced, that we resent injuries, or make preparation for our defence. With the movements in this hemisphere we are, of necessity, more immediately connected, and by causes which must be obvious to all enlightened and impartial observers. The political system of the allied powers is essentially different in this respect from that of America. This difference proceeds from that which exists in their respective governments; and to the defence of our own, which has been achieved by the loss of so much blood and treasure, and matured by the wisdom of our most enlightened citizens, and under which we have enjoyed unexampled felicity, this whole nation is devoted. We owe it, therefore, to candor, and to the amicable relations existing between the United States and those powers, to declare that we should consider any attempt on their part to extend their system to any portion of this hemisphere as dangerous to our peace and safety. With the existing colonies, or dependencies, of any European power, we have not interfered, and shall not interfere; but with the governments who have declared their independence and maintained it, and whose independence we have, on great consideration and on just principles, acknowledged, we could not view any interposition for the purpose of oppressing them, or controlling in any other manner their destiny, by any European power, in any other light than as the manifestation of an unfriendly disposition towards the United States." *

1824. — Dec. 7. The last message of Monroe to Congress, after alluding to the continued growth and prosperity of the nation, the visit of Lafayette, &c., closes as follows: "I cannot conclude this communication, the last of the kind which I shall have to make, without recollecting with great sensibility and heartfelt gratitude the many instances of the public confidence and the

---

* "The Monroe Doctrine," it is believed, was suggested by John Quincy Adams, Secretary of State under Monroe.

generous support which I have received from my fellow-citizens in the various trusts with which I have been honored. Having commenced my service in early youth, and continued it since, with few and short intervals, I have witnessed the great difficulties to which our Union has been exposed, and admired the virtue and courage with which they were surmounted. From the present prosperous and happy state I derive a gratification which I cannot express. That these blessings may be preserved and perpetuated will be the object of my fervent and unceasing prayers to the Supreme Ruler of the universe. .

"JAMES MONROE."

Q. ADAMS'S ADMINISTRATION.

1825 TO 1829.

THE CABINET.

PRESIDENT:
JOHN QUINCY ADAMS, MASSACHUSETTS.

VICE-PRESIDENT:
JOHN C. CALHOUN, SOUTH CAROLINA.

SECRETARY OF STATE:
1825.— HENRY CLAY, Kentucky.

SECRETARY OF THE TREASURY:
1825.— RICHARD RUSH, Pennsylvania.

SECRETARIES OF WAR:
1825.— JAMES BARBOUR, Virginia.
1828.— PETER B. PORTER, New York.

SECRETARY OF THE NAVY:
1825.— SAMUEL L. SOUTHARD, New Jersey.

POSTMASTER-GENERAL:
1825.— JOHN MCLEAN, Ohio.

ATTORNEY-GENERAL:
1825.— WILLIAM WIRT, Virginia.

CONTEMPORANEOUS ENGLISH HISTORY.

George IV., King of England.
Lord Liverpool, Prime-Minister, 1812 to 1827.
Mr. Canning, Lord Goderich, and the Duke of Wellington, to 1830.
Great monetary crisis in 1825.
Suspension of seventy banks in December.
The Bank of England, with difficulty, weathers the storm.
Sir Walter Scott's influence secures the circulation of small notes in Scotland.
Independence of South-American States recognized.
Death of Lord Liverpool, Dec. 4, 1828.

JOHN QUINCY ADAMS.

FROM — 1825 to 1829.
DURATION. — One term, — four years.
PARTY. — Republican.
PRINCIPAL EVENTS. — Remarkable prosperity in agriculture, commerce, and manufactures. Extensive internal improvements. Quincy Railway finished for the transportation of granite to the seashore. This was the first railroad built in the United States: locomotives afterwards introduced on the Hudson and Mohawk Railroad. Duel between Clay and Randolph, April 8, 1826; two shots and a reconciliation. Continued commercial prosperity. Commerce and shipping gradually turning from Boston to New York. John Adams and Thomas Jefferson pass away on the same day; namely, July 4, 1826, — the fiftieth anniversary of American Independence. New party organized excluding Free Masons from office; its failure. Erie Canal finished by the State of New York. Exciting Congressional discussions over the protective tariff bill. New England, compelled to adopt it by the vote of the South during the Monroe administration, now refuses to change. Webster favors protection. Bitter party-spirit, resulting in the defeat of John Quincy Adams on his second nomination. Election of Gen. Andrew Jackson.

1825. — March 4. "In compliance with an usage co-eval with the existence of our Federal

Constitution, and sanctioned by the example of my predecessors in the career upon which I am about to enter, I appear, my fellow-citizens, in your presence and in that of Heaven, to bind myself by the solemnity of religious obligation to the faithful performance of the duties allotted to me in the situation to which I have been called. . . . Union, justice, tranquillity, the common defence, the general welfare, and the blessings of liberty, — all have been promoted by the government under which we have lived. . . . If there have been projects of partial confederacies to be erected on the ruins of the Union, they have been scattered to the winds. . . . To the topic of internal improvements, emphatically urged by my predecessor at his inauguration, I recur with peculiar satisfaction. It is that from which I am convinced that the unborn millions of our posterity who are in future ages to people this continent will derive their most fervent gratitude to the founders of the Union; that in which the beneficent action of its government will be most deeply felt and acknowledged. The magnificence and splendor of their public works are among the imperishable glories of the ancient republics. The roads and aqueducts of Rome have been the admiration of all after-ages, and have survived thousands of years, — after all her conquests have been swallowed up in despotism, or become the spoil of barbarians. Some diversity of opinion has prevailed with regard to the powers of Congress. for legislation upon objects of this nature. The most respectful deference is due to doubts originating in pure patriotism, and sustained by venerated authority. But nearly twenty years have passed since the construction of the first national road was commenced. The authority for its construction was then unquestioned. To how many thousands of our countrymen has it proved a benefit! To what single individual has it ever proved an injury?" . . .

1825. — Dec. 6. "Europe, with a few partial and unhappy exceptions, has enjoyed ten years of peace. . . . During the same period, our intercourse with all those nations has been pacific and friendly: it so continues. . . . The policy of the United States, in their commercial intercourse with other nations, has always been of the most liberal character. . . . Among the unequivocal indications of our national prosperity is the flourishing state of our finances. . . . Our relations with the numerous tribes of aboriginal natives of this country have been, during the present year, highly interesting. . . . The acts of Congress of the last session, relative to the surveying, marking, or laying-out roads in the Territories of Florida, Arkansas, and Michigan, from Missouri to Mexico, and for the continuation of the Cumberland Road, are some of them fully executed, and others in the process of execution." . . . Respecting the establishment of an astronomical observatory he says, "It is with no feeling of pride as an American that the remark may be made, that, on the comparatively small territorial surface of Europe, there are existing upwards of a hundred and thirty of these lighthouses of the skies; while throughout the whole American hemisphere there is not one." . . .

1826. — Dec. 9. "With the exceptions incidental to the most felicitous condition of human existence, we continue to be highly favored in all the elements which contribute to individual comfort and to national prosperity. . . . In our intercourse with the other nations of the earth, we have still the happiness of enjoying peace and a general good understanding. . . . By the decease of the Emperor Alexander of Russia, which occurred contemporaneously with the commencement of the last session of Congress, the United States have been deprived of a long-tried, steady, and faithful friend." . . .

1827.—Dec. 8. "Peace and prosperity prevail to a degree seldom experienced over the whole habitable globe; presenting, though as yet with painful exceptions, a foretaste of that blessed period of promise, when the lion shall lie down with the lamb, and wars shall be no more. . . . Our relations of friendship with the other nations of the earth, political and commercial, have been preserved unimpaired, and the opportunities to improve them have been cultivated with anxious and unremitting attention. . . . In the American hemisphere, the cause of freedom and independence has continued to prevail; and, if signalized by none of those splendid triumphs which had crowned with glory some of the preceding years, it has only been from the banishment of all external force against which the struggle had been maintained. . . . The deep solicitude felt by our citizens of all classes throughout the Union for the total discharge of the public debt will apologize for the earnestness with which I deem it my duty to urge this topic upon the consideration of Congress."

1828.—Dec. 2. "If the enjoyment in profusion of the bounties of Providence forms a suitable subject of mutual gratulation and grateful acknowledgment, we are admonished at this return of the season, when the representatives of the nation are assembled to deliberate upon their concerns, to offer up the tribute of fervent and grateful hearts for the never-failing mercies of Him who ruleth over all. He has again favored us with healthful seasons and abundant harvests. He has sustained us at peace with foreign countries, and in tranquillity within our borders. He has preserved us in the quiet and undisturbed possession of civil and religious liberty. He has crowned the year with his goodness, imposing on us no other conditions than of improving for our own happiness the blessings bestowed by his hands; and, in the fruition of all his favors, of devoting the faculties with which we have been endowed by him to his glory and to our own temporal and eternal welfare." . . .

"JOHN QUINCY ADAMS."

JACKSON'S ADMINISTRATION.

1829 TO 1837.

THE CABINET.

PRESIDENT:
ANDREW JACKSON, Tennessee.

VICE-PRESIDENTS:
JOHN C. CALHOUN, South Carolina.
MARTIN VAN BUREN, New York.

SECRETARIES OF STATE:
1829. — Martin Van Buren, New York.
1831. — Edward Livingston, Louisiana.
1833. — Louis McLane, Delaware.
1834. — John Forsyth, Georgia.

SECRETARIES OF THE TREASURY:
1829. — Samuel D. Ingham, Pennsylvania.
1831. — Louis McLane, Delaware.
1833. — William J. Duane, Pennsylvania.
1833. — Roger B. Taney, Maryland.
1834. — Levi Woodbury, New Hampshire.

SECRETARIES OF WAR:
1829. — John H. Eaton, Tennessee.
1831. — Lewis Cass, Ohio.

SECRETARIES OF THE NAVY:
1829. — John Branch, North Carolina.
1831. — Levi Woodbury, New Hampshire.
1834. — Mahlon Dickerson, New Jersey.

POSTMASTERS-GENERAL:
1829. — William T. Barry, Kentucky.
1835. — Amos Kendall, Kentucky.

ATTORNEYS-GENERAL:
1829. — John M. Berrien, Georgia.
1831. — Roger B. Taney, Maryland.
1834. — Benjamin F. Butler, New York.

CONTEMPORANEOUS ENGLISH HISTORY.

George IV. and William IV.
Duke of Wellington Prime-Minister, 1828 to 1830.
Earl Gray, Lord Melbourne, and Sir Robert Peel, 1830 to 1837.
Catholic-Emancipation Riots.
Death of George IV., July, 1830.
Revolution in Paris, July 27, 1830. Charles X. abdicates; and the Duke of Orléans, as Louis Philippe, ascends the throne.

ANDREW JACKSON.

FROM — 1829 to 1837.

DURATION. — Two terms, — eight years.

PARTY. — Democratic.

PRINCIPAL EVENTS. — Attempted "REFORM." Removals from office to secure the services of political friends (six hundred and ninety removals in eight years to sixty-four in forty-four years). Postmaster-General for the first time admitted to the cabinet. Cherokees removed from Georgia. Two missionaries imprisoned. Their release procured by Chief Justice Marshall. They follow the Indians. In 1830, Webster replies to Hayne of South Carolina on the Foot "*Resolution of inquiry as to the disposal of public lands.*" Nullification openly avowed in Congress. John C. Calhoun, leader of the South-Carolina State-rights nullification party, resigns the Vice-Presidency of the United States, and in the Senate declares the protective tariff (originally introduced by the South) null and void, and threatens secession, if the Union, by force, endeavors to execute it in South Carolina. Jackson, resolved to enforce it, sends a national vessel and troops to Charleston to aid the officers in the collection of revenue. Henry Clay introduces a compromise, and the matter is temporarily adjusted. Black-Hawk War in Illinois and Wisconsin. Black Hawk is captured, and carried through the principal Eastern cities. Re-charter of the United-States Bank vetoed by Jackson. The Seven-Years' Florida War with the Seminoles commenced in 1835. Osceola and the other Indians would not be removed beyond the Mississippi River. Col. Zachary Taylor finally forces submission, and closes the war. Arkansas admitted in 1836, and Michigan in 1837. Party-lines distinctly drawn. Supporters of the administration (opposed to a United-States Bank and the protective tariff) are called Democrats; all others, Whigs. Election of Martin Van Buren.

1829.— March 4. "About to undertake the arduous duties that I have been appointed to perform by the choice of a free people, I avail myself of this customary and solemn occasion to express the gratitude which their confidence inspires, and to acknowledge the accountability which my situation enjoins. . . . As the instrument of the Federal Constitution, it will devolve upon me, for a stated period, to execute the laws of the United States, to superintend their foreign and confederate relations, to manage their revenue, to command their forces, and, by communications to the Legislature, to watch over and to promote their interests generally. . . . The recent demonstration of public sentiment inscribes on the list of executive duties, in characters too legible to be overlooked, the task of REFORM. . . . A firm reliance on the goodness of that Power whose providence mercifully protected our national infancy, and has since upheld our liberties in various vicissitudes, encourages me to offer up my ardent supplications that he will continue to make our beloved country the object of his divine care and gracious benediction."

1829. — Dec. 8. "The task devolves on me, under a provision of the Constitution, to present to you, as the Federal Legislature of twenty-four sovereign States and twelve millions of happy people, a view of our affairs. . . . In communicating with you for the first time, it is to me a source of unfeigned satisfaction, calling for mutual gratulation and devout thanks to a benign Providence, that we are at peace with all mankind, and that our country exhibits the most cheering evidence of general welfare and progressive improvement. Turning our eyes to other nations, our great desire is to see our brethren of the human race secured in the blessings enjoyed by ourselves, and advancing in knowledge, in freedom, and in social happiness. . . . Of the unsettled matters between the United States and other powers, the most prominent are those which have for years been the subject of negotiation with England, France, and Spain. With Great Britain, alike distinguished in peace and war, we may look forward to years of peaceful, honorable, and elevated competition. Every thing in the condition and history of the two nations is calculated to inspire sentiments of mutual respect, and to carry conviction to the minds of both that it is their policy to preserve the most cordial relations. From France, our ancient ally, we have a right to expect that justice which becomes the sovereign of a powerful, intelligent, and magnanimous people. . . . The claims of our citizens for depredations upon their property, long since committed under the authority, and in many instances by the express direction, of the then-existing government of France, remain unsatisfied, and must therefore continue to furnish a subject of unpleasant discussion and possible collision between the two governments. . . . Our minister recently appointed to Spain has been authorized to assist in removing evils alike injurious to both countries. . . . With other European powers our intercourse is on the most friendly footing.

"The recent invasion of Mexico must have a

controlling influence upon the great questions of South-American emancipation. . . . Prejudices long indulged by a portion of the inhabitants of Mexico against the envoy-extraordinary and minister-plenipotentary of the United States have had an unfortunate influence upon the affairs of the two countries. . . . I consider it one of the most urgent of my duties to bring to your attention the propriety of amending that part of our Constitution which relates to the election of a President and Vice-President. To the people belongs the right of electing their chief magistrate: it was never designed that their choice should, in any case, be defeated either by the intervention of electoral colleges, or by the agency confided, under certain contingencies, to the House of Representatives. Experience proves, that, in proportion as agents to execute the will of the people are multiplied, there is danger of their wishes being frustrated. Some may be unfaithful. All are liable to err. So far, therefore, as the people can with convenience speak, it is safer for them to express their own will."

1830. — Dec. 7. "The importance of the

principle involved in the inquiry, whether it will be proper to re-charter the Bank of the United States, requires that I should again call the attention of Congress to the subject. Nothing has occurred to lessen in any degree the dangers which many of our citizens apprehended from that institution as at present organized. In the spirit of improvement and compromise which distinguishes our country and its institutions, it becomes us to inquire whether it be not possible to secure the advantages afforded by the present bank through the agency of a Bank of the United States so modified in its principles and structure as to obviate constitutional and other objections." . . .

1831.—Dec. 6. "For near half a century, the chief magistrates who have been successively chosen have made their annual communications of the state of the nation to its representatives. But, frequently and justly as you have been called on to be grateful for the bounties of Providence, at few periods have they been more abundantly or extensively bestowed than at the present; rarely, if ever, have we had greater reason to congratulate each other on the continued and increasing prosperity of our beloved country." . . .

1832. — July 10. Bank-veto Message.

Dec. 4. Fourth Annual Message. "Although the pestilence which had traversed the Old World has entered our limits, and extended its ravages over much of our land, it has pleased Almighty God to mitigate its severity, and lessen the number of victims, compared with those who have fallen in most other countries over which it has spread its terrors. Notwithstanding this visitation, our country presents on every side marks of prosperity and happiness, unequalled, perhaps, in any other portion of the world." . . .

Dec. 11. Proclamation. "I, Andrew Jackson, President of the United States, have thought proper to issue this my PROCLAMATION, stating my views of the Constitution and laws applicable to the measures adopted by the Convention of South Carolina. . . . If South Carolina considers the revenue-laws unconstitutional, and has a right to prevent their execution in the port of Charleston, there would be a clear constitutional objection to their collection in every other port, and no revenue could be collected anywhere; for all impost must be equal." . . .

1833.—Jan. 16. Nullification Message. "A recent proclamation of the present governor of South Carolina has openly defied the authority of the Executive of the Union; and general orders from the headquarters of the State announce his determination to accept the services of volunteers, and his belief, that, should their country need their services, they will be found at the post of honor and duty, ready to lay down their lives in her defence. Under these orders, the forces referred to are directed to 'hold themselves in readiness to take the field at a moment's warning;' and in the city of Charleston, within a collection district and a port of entry, a rendezvous has been opened for the purpose of enlisting men for the magazine and municipal guard. Thus South Carolina presents herself in the attitude of hostile preparation, and ready even for military violence, if need be, to enforce her laws for preventing the collection of the duties within her limits. . . . I fervently pray that the great Ruler of nations may so guide your deliberations and our joint measures, as that they may prove salutary examples, not only to the present, but to future times; and solemnly proclaim that the Constitution and the laws are supreme, and the *Union indissoluble.*" . . .

1833.—March 4. Second Inaugural Address. "The time at which I stand before you is full of interest. The eyes of all nations are fixed upon our republic. The event of the existing crisis will be decisive, in the opinion of mankind, of the practicability of our federal system of government. Great is the stake placed in our hands; great is the responsibility which must rest upon the people of the United States. Let us realize the importance of the attitude in which we stand before the world; let us exercise forbearance and firmness; let us extricate our country from the dangers which surround it, and learn wisdom from the lessons they inculcate. . . . Finally, it is my most fervent prayer to that Almighty Being before whom I now stand, and who has kept us in his hands from the infancy of our republic to the present day, that he will so overrule all my intentions and actions, and inspire the hearts of my fellow-citizens, that we may be preserved from dangers of all kinds, and continue forever a UNITED AND HAPPY PEOPLE."

1834.—April 15. Jackson's protest. "It appears by the published journal of the Senate, that, on the 26th of December last, a resolution was offered by a member of the Senate, which, after a protracted debate, was, on the twenty-eighth day of March last, modified by the mover, and passed by the votes of twenty-six senators out of forty-six, who were present and voted, in the following words: —

"'*Resolved*, That the President, in the late executive proceedings in relation to the public revenue, has assumed upon himself authority and power not conferred by the Constitution and laws, but in derogation of both.' . . . Having had the honor, through the voluntary suffrages of the American people, to fill the office of President of the United States during the period which may be presumed to have been referred to in this resolution, it is sufficiently evident that the censure it inflicts was intended for myself. Without notice, unheard and untried, I thus find myself charged on the records of the Senate, and in a form hitherto unknown in our history, with the high crime of violating the laws and Constitution of my country. . . . It cannot be doubted that it was the legal duty of the Secretary of the Treasury to order and direct the deposits of the public money to be made elsewhere than in the Bank of the United States, *whenever sufficient reasons existed for making the change.* . . . The dangerous tendency of the doctrine which denies to the President the power of supervising, directing, and removing the Secretary of the Treasury in like manner with other executive officers would soon be manifest in practice were the doctrine to be established. The President is the direct representative of the American people; but the secretaries are not." . . .

1834.—June 21. "The afflicting intelligence of the death of the illustrious Lafayette has been received by me this morning." . . .

Dec. 2. Annual Message. "Events have satisfied my mind, and I think the minds of the American people, that the mischiefs and dangers which flow from a national bank far overbalance all its advantages. . . . The State banks are found fully adequate to the performance of all services which were required of the Bank of the United States, quite as promptly, and with the same cheapness." . . .

1835.—Dec. 2. "Never, in any former period of our history, have we had greater reason than we now have to be thankful to Divine Providence for the blessings of health and general prosperity. Every branch of labor we see crowned with the most abundant rewards: in every element of national resources and wealth, and of individual comfort, we witness the most rapid and solid improvements. . . . It has been seen, that, without the agency of a great moneyed monopoly, the revenue can be collected, and conveniently and safely applied to all the purposes of the public expenditure."

1836.—Feb. 8. "The government of Great Britain has offered its mediation for the adjustment of the dispute between the United States and France." . . .

May 10. "Information has been received at the treasury department, that the four instalments under our treaty with France have been paid to the agent of the United States. In communicating this satisfactory termination of our controversy with France, I feel assured that both houses of Congress will unite with me in desiring and believing that the anticipations of a restoration of the ancient cordial relations between the two countries, expressed in my former message on this subject, will be speedily realized."

1836. — Dec. 6. "Addressing to you the last Annual Message I shall ever present to the Congress of the United States, it is a source of the most heartfelt satisfaction to be able to congratulate you on the high state of prosperity which our beloved country has attained. With no causes at home or abroad to lessen the confidence with which we look to the future for continuing proofs of the capacity of our free institutions to produce all the fruits of good government, the general condition of our affairs may well excite our national pride. . . . All that has occurred during my administration is calculated to inspire me with increased confidence in the stability of our institutions; and should I be spared to enter upon that retirement which is so suitable to my age and infirm health, and so much desired by me in other respects, I shall not cease to invoke that beneficent Being, to whose providence we are already so signally indebted, for the continuance of his blessings on our beloved country."

1837.—March 3. Closing passages of the Farewell Address: "The progress of the United States under our free and happy institutions has surpassed the most sanguine hopes of the founders of the republic. Our growth has been rapid beyond all former example, in numbers, in wealth, in knowledge, and all the useful arts which contribute to the comforts and convenience of man; and, from the earliest ages of history to the present day, there never have been thirteen millions of people, associated together in one political body, who enjoyed so much freedom and happiness as the people of these United States. You have no longer any cause to fear danger from abroad; your strength and power are well known throughout the civilized world, as well as the high and gallant bearing of your sons. It is from within, among yourselves, from cupidity, from corruption, from disappointed ambition, and inordinate thirst for power, that factions will be formed, and liberty endangered. . . . You have the highest of human trusts committed to your care. Providence has showered on this favored land blessings without number, and has chosen you, as the guardians of freedom, to preserve it for the benefit of the human race. May He who holds in his hands the destinies of nations make you worthy of the favors he has bestowed, and enable you, with pure hearts and pure hands, and sleepless vigilance, to guard and defend to the end of time the great charge he has committed to your keeping! . . . I thank God that my life has been spent in a land of liberty, and that he has given me a heart to love my country with the affection of a son. And, filled with gratitude for your constant and unwavering kindness, I bid you a last and affectionate farewell. "ANDREW JACKSON."

VAN BUREN'S ADMINISTRATION.

1837 TO 1841.

THE CABINET.

PRESIDENT:
MARTIN VAN BUREN, NEW YORK.

VICE-PRESIDENT:
RICHARD M. JOHNSON, KENTUCKY.

SECRETARY OF STATE:
1837.— JOHN FORSYTH, Georgia.

SECRETARY OF THE TREASURY:
1837.— LEVI WOODBURY, New Hampshire.

SECRETARY OF WAR:
1837.— JOEL R. POINSETT, South Carolina.

SECRETARIES OF THE NAVY:
1837.— MAHLON DICKERSON, New Jersey.
1838.— JAMES K. PAULDING, New York.

POSTMASTERS-GENERAL:
1837.— AMOS KENDALL, Kentucky.
1840.— JOHN M. NILES, Connecticut.

ATTORNEYS-GENERAL:
1837.— BENJAMIN F. BUTLER, New York.
1838.— FELIX GRUNDY, Tennessee.
1840.— HENRY D. GILPIN, Pennsylvania.

CONTEMPORANEOUS ENGLISH HISTORY.

Reign — William IV. and Victoria.
Lord Melbourne Prime-Minister (second time).
Commercial failures.
King William IV. died June 20, 1837.
Queen Victoria ascended the throne.
Coronation, June 28, 1838.
Rebellion in Canada in 1838 on account of British taxation and expenditures.
Affghan War in India
Another rebellion in Canada in 1839.
Disturbances in Ireland. The Corn Laws, instead of the Irish Church, the party question.
Chartist riots at Birmingham and elsewhere.
Penny-postage established in 1840.
Marriage of the Queen and Prince Albert, Feb. 10, 1840.
Upper and Lower Canada one government.
Chinese War.

MARTIN VAN BUREN.

FROM — 1837 to 1841.

DURATION. — One term, — four years.

PARTY. — Democratic.

PRINCIPAL EVENTS. — Relations with England disturbed by a rebellion in Canada for independence. The supply steamboat "Caroline," owned by American adventurers, is seized by British authorities, fired, and sent in flames over Niagara Falls. McLeod is arrested and acquitted. Terrible financial disasters. Nearly a thousand banks engaged in land-speculations, amounting to millions monthly. Prospective cities, towns, and villages elegantly laid out *on paper*. Suspension of State banks. More mercantile failures in 1837 than in any previous year of the republic. The United-States Bank suspends specie payment, Oct. 9, 1839. Mississippi, and Florida Territory, repudiate their debts. An independent United-States Treasury, with sub-treasury offices in New York and other ports of collection, is organized in 1839. The Republic of Texas applies for admission to the Union. Another slavery agitation. Debate between Clay and Calhoun. North-eastern boundary question settled in 1840 (line subsequently adjusted by Lord Ashburton and Daniel Webster). Lieut. Wilkes's exploring-expedition is on its way to the Arctic regions. Gen. William Henry Harrison is elected President.

1837. — March 4. Extracts from the Inaugural Address: "The last, perhaps the greatest, of the prominent sources of discord and disaster supposed to lurk in our political condition was the institution of domestic slavery. Our forefathers were deeply impressed with the delicacy of this subject; and they treated it with a forbearance so evidently wise, that, in spite of every sinister foreboding, it never, until the present period, disturbed the tranquillity of our common country. . . . I must go into the presidential chair the inflexible and uncompromising opponent of every attempt on the part of Congress to abolish slavery in the District of Columbia against the wishes of the slaveholding States; and also with a determination, equally decided, to resist the slightest interference with it in the States where it exists." . . .

1837.—Sept. 4. "Banking has become a political topic of the highest interest; and trade has suffered in the conflict of parties. . . . My own views upon the subject have been repeatedly and unreservedly announced to my fellow-citizens, who, with full knowledge of them, conferred upon me the two highest offices of the government. On the last of these occasions, I felt it due to the people to apprise them distinctly, that, in the event of my election, I would not be able to co-operate in the re-establishment of a national bank. . . . The suspension of specie payments at such a time, and under such circumstances as we have lately witnessed, could not be other than a temporary measure ; and we can scarcely err in believing that the period must soon arrive when all that are solvent will redeem their issues in gold and silver.". . . .

1837.—Dec. 4. First Annual Message. "We have reason to renew the expression of our devout gratitude to the Giver of all good for his benign protection. Our country presents on every side the evidences of that continued favor under whose auspices it has gradually risen from a few feeble and dependent colonies to a prosperous and powerful confederacy. We are blessed with domestic tranquillity and all the elements of national prosperity. The pestilence, which, invading for a time some flourishing portions of our Union, interrupted the general prevalence of unusual health, has, happily, been limited in extent, and arrested in its fatal career. The industry and prudence of our citizens are gradually relieving them from the pecuniary embarrassments under which portions of them have labored; judicious legislation and the natural and boundless resources of the country have afforded wise and timely aid to private enterprise; and the activity always characteristic of our people has already, in a great degree, resumed its usual and profitable channels. We remain at peace with all nations; and no effort on my part, consistent with the preservation of our rights and the honor of our country, shall be spared to maintain a position so consonant to our institutions. . . . Of pending questions, the most important is that which exists with the government of Great Britain in respect to our northeastern boundary. It is with unfeigned regret that the people of the United States must look back upon the abortive efforts made by the Executive, for a period of more than half a century, to determine what no nation should suffer long to remain in dispute, — the true line which divides its possessions from those of other powers. . . . Civil war yet rages in Spain, producing intense suffering to its own people, and to other nations inconvenience and regret. . . . Notwithstanding the great embarrassments which have recently occurred in commercial affairs, it is gratifying to be able to anticipate that the treasury-notes which have been issued during the present year will be redeemed, and that the resources of the treasury, without any resort to loans or increased taxes, will prove ample for defraying all charges imposed on it during 1838. . . . The system of removing the Indians west of the Mississippi, commenced by Mr. Jefferson in 1804, has been steadily persevered in by every succeeding president, and may be considered the settled policy of the country."

1838. — Dec. 4. Second Annual Message. "I congratulate you on the favorable circumstances in the condition of our country under which you re-assemble for the performance of your official duties. . . . These blessings, which evince the care and beneficence of Providence, call for our devout and fervent gratitude. . . . The most amicable dispositions continue to be exhibited by all the nations with whom the government and citizens of the United States have an habitual intercourse. At the date of my last Annual

Message, Mexico was the only nation which could not be included in so gratifying a reference to our foreign relations." . . . Respecting the Canadian rebellion he says, "If an insurrection existed in Canada, the amicable dispositions of the United States toward Great Britain, as well as their duty to themselves, would lead them to maintain a strict neutrality, and to restrain their citizens from all violations of the laws which have been passed for its enforcement."

1839.—Dec. 24. "I regret that I cannot, on this occasion, congratulate you that the past year has been one of unalloyed prosperity. The ravages of fire and disease have painfully afflicted otherwise flourishing portions of our country, and serious embarrassments yet derange the trade of many of our cities; but, notwithstanding these adverse circumstances, that general prosperity which has been heretofore so bountifully bestowed upon us by the Author of all good still continues to call for our warmest gratitude." . . .

1840.—Dec. 5. Fourth Annual Message. "Our devout gratitude is due to the Supreme Being for having graciously continued to our beloved country, through the vicissitudes of another year, the invaluable blessings of health, plenty, and peace. Seldom has this favored land been so generally exempted from the ravages of disease, or the labor of the husbandman been more amply rewarded; and never before have our relations with other countries been placed on a more favorable basis. . . . With Austria, France, Prussia, Russia, and the remaining powers of Europe, our relations continue to be of the most friendly character. . . . The industry, enterprise, perseverance, and economy of the American people cannot fail to raise the whole country at an early period to a state of solid and enduring prosperity, not subject to be again overthrown by the suspension of banks or the explosion of a bloated credit-system. It is for the people and their representatives to decide whether or not the permanent welfare of the country, which all good citizens equally desire, however widely they may differ as to the means of its accomplishment, shall be in this way secured. . . .   "MARTIN VAN BUREN."

ADMINISTRATIONS

OF

W. H. HARRISON AND J. TYLER.

1841 TO 1845.

THE CABINET.

PRESIDENTS:
WILLIAM HENRY HARRISON, Ohio,
(Died April 4, 1841.)
JOHN TYLER, Virginia.

VICE-PRESIDENT:
JOHN TYLER, Virginia.

SECRETARIES OF STATE:
1841. — Daniel Webster, Massachusetts.
1843. — Hugh S. Légaré, South Carolina.
1843. — Abel P. Upshur, Virginia.
1844. — John Nelson, Maryland.
1845. — John C. Calhoun, South Carolina.

SECRETARIES OF THE TREASURY:
1841. — Thomas Ewing, Ohio.
1841. — Walter Forward, Pennsylvania.
1843. — J. C. Spencer, New York.
1844. — George M. Bibb, Kentucky.

SECRETARIES OF WAR:
1841. — John Bell, Tennessee.
1841. — John C. Spencer, New York.
1843. — James M. Porter, Pennsylvania.
1844. — William Wilkins, Pennsylvania.

SECRETARIES OF THE NAVY:
1841. — George E. Badger, North Carolina.
1841. — Abel P. Upshur, Virginia.
1843. — David Henshaw, Massachusetts.
1844. — Thomas W. Gilmer, Virginia.
1844. — John Y. Mason, Virginia.

POSTMASTERS-GENERAL:
1841. — Francis Granger, New York.
1841. — Charles A. Wickliffe, Kentucky.

ATTORNEYS-GENERAL:
1841. — John J. Crittenden, Kentucky.
1841. — Hugh S. Légaré, South Carolina.
1844. — John Nelson, Maryland.

CONTEMPORANEOUS ENGLISH HISTORY.
Reign. — Victoria.
Lord Melbourne, Prime-Minister.
Resignation of the ministry, Aug. 30, 1841.
Sir Robert Peel, Premier, from Sept. 8, 1841, to 1846.
Affghan War in India. Bank Charter Act. Repeal of Corn Laws.
Chinese War ended in 1842.
National distress and commercial disasters in 1843.

WILLIAM HENRY HARRISON AND JOHN TYLER.

FROM — March 4, 1841, to 1845.

DURATION. — One term, — four years.

PARTY. — Whig.

PRINCIPAL EVENTS. — Death of Harrison one month after his inauguration. John Tyler, as Vice-President, inaugurated President. Sub-treasury Law repealed Aug. 9, 1841. A general Bankrupt Law passed. "The Fiscal Bank of the United States" Bill vetoed Aug. 16. "The Fiscal Corporation of the United States" Bill vetoed Sept. 9. Whig party furious. General dissolution of the cabinet. Daniel Webster the last to resign. Lord Ashburton Treaty signed. Rhode-Island Dorr Rebellion, resulting in a new constitution in place of the Charles II. charter. Oregon question introduced. Liberty party organized. Treaty arranged with China by Caleb Cushing. The Mormon Joe Smith and his brother murdered by a mob. Resolution of Congress for the annexation of Texas signed by Pres. Tyler, March 1, 1845; also bills admitting Florida and Iowa. Emigration westward constantly increasing. James K. Polk elected President.

1841. — March 4. Extracts from the Inaugural Address of William Henry Harrison: " Called from a retirement, which I had supposed was to continue for the residue of my life, to fill the chief executive office of this great and free nation, I appear before you, fellow-citizens, to take the oath which the Constitution prescribes as a necessary qualification for the performance of its duties. . . . However strong may be my present purpose to realize the expectations of a magnanimous and confiding people, I too well understand the infirmities of human nature, and the dangers and temptations to which I shall be exposed, not to place my chief confidence upon the aid of that Almighty Power which has hitherto protected me, and enabled me to bring to favorable issues other important but still greatly-inferior trusts heretofore confided to me by my country. . . . We admit of no government by divine right; believing that, so far as power is concerned, the beneficent Creator has made no distinction among men; that all are upon an equality; and that the only legitimate right to govern is an express grant of power from the governed. The Constitution of the United States is the instrument containing the grant of power to the several departments composing the government. . . . The great danger to our institutions does not appear to me to be in a usurpation by the government of power not granted by the people, but by the accumulation in one of the departments of that which was assigned to others. Limited as are powers which have been granted, still enough have been granted to constitute a despotism, if concentrated in one of the departments. . . . Of the eligibility of the same individual to a second term of the presidency, the sagacious mind of Mr. Jefferson early saw and lamented the error; and attempts have been made, hitherto without success, to apply the amendatory power of the States to its correction. As, however, one mode of correction is in the power of every President, and consequently in mine, it would be useless, and perhaps invidious, to enumerate the evils, of which, in the opinion of many of our fellow-citizens, this error of the sages who framed the Constitution may have been the source, and the bitter fruits which we are still to gather from it if it continues to disfigure our system. It may be observed, however, as a general remark, that republics can commit no greater error than to adopt or continue any feature in their systems of government which may be calculated to create or increase the love of power in the bosoms of those to whom necessity obliges them to commit the management of their affairs. And surely nothing is more likely to produce such a state of mind than the long continuance of an office of high trust; nothing can be more corrupting, nothing more destructive of all those noble feelings which belong to the character of a devoted republican patriot. When this corrupting passion once takes possession of the human mind, like the love of gold, it becomes insatiable: it is the never-dying worm in his bosom; grows with his growth, and strengthens with the declining years of its victim. If this is true, it is the part of wisdom for a republic to limit the service of that officer, at least, to whom she has intrusted the management of her foreign relations, the execution of her laws, and the command of her armies and navies, to a period so short as to prevent his forgetting that he is the accountable agent, not the principal; the servant, not the master. Until an amendment of the Constitution can be effected, public opinion may secure the desired object. I give my aid to it by renewing the pledge heretofore given, that under no circumstances will I consent to serve a second term. . . . There is no part of the means placed in the hands of the Executive which might be used with greater effect for unhallowed purposes than the control of the public press. The maxim which our ancestors derived from the mother-country, that 'the freedom of the press is the great bulwark of civil and religious liberty,' is one of the most precious legacies which they left us. We have learned too, from our own as well as the experience of other countries, that golden shackles, by whomsoever, or by whatever pretence, imposed, are as fatal to it as the iron bonds of despotism. The presses in the necessary employment of the government should never be used 'to clear the guilty, or to varnish crimes.' A decent and manly examination of the acts of the government should be not only tolerated, but encouraged. Upon another occasion, I have given my opinion, at some length, upon the impropriety of executive interference in the legislation of Congress. . . . In our intercourse with our aboriginal neighbors, the same liberality and justice which marked the course prescribed to me by two of my illustrious predecessors, when acting under their direction in the discharge of the duties of superintendent and commissioner, shall be strictly observed. I can conceive of no more sublime spectacle — none more likely to propitiate an impartial Creator — than a rigid adherence to the principles of justice on the part of a powerful nation in its transactions with a weaker and uncivilized people whom circumstances have placed at its disposal. . . . Always the friend of my countrymen, never their flatterer, it becomes my duty to say to them from this high place to which their partiality has exalted me, that there exists in the land a spirit hostile to their best interests, hostile to liberty itself. It is a spirit contracted in its views, selfish in its object: it looks to the aggrandizement of a few, even to the destruction of the interest of the whole. The entire remedy is with the people. Something, however, may be effected by the means which they have placed in my hands. It is union that we want, — not of a party for the sake of party, but a union of the whole country for the sake of the whole country. . . . I deem the present occasion sufficiently important and solemn to justify me in expressing to my fellow-citizens a profound reverence for the Christian religion, and a thorough conviction that sound morals, religious liberty, and a just sense of religious responsibility, are essentially connected with all true and lasting happiness. And to that good Being who has blessed us by the gifts of civil and religious freedom, who watched over and prospered the labors of our fathers, and has hitherto preserved to us institutions far exceeding in excellence those of any other people, let us unite in fervently commending every interest of our beloved country in all future time.

"WILLIAM HENRY HARRISON."

POLK'S ADMINISTRATION.

1845 TO 1849.

THE CABINET.

PRESIDENT:
JAMES KNOX POLK, TENNESSEE.
VICE-PRESIDENT:
GEORGE M. DALLAS, PENNSYLVANIA.
SECRETARY OF STATE:
1845.—JAMES BUCHANAN, Pennsylvania.
SECRETARY OF THE TREASURY:
1845.—ROBERT J. WALKER, Mississippi.
SECRETARY OF WAR:
1845.—WILLIAM L. MARCY, New York.
SECRETARIES OF THE NAVY:
1845.—GEORGE BANCROFT, Massachusetts.
1846.—JOHN Y. MASON, Virginia.
POSTMASTER-GENERAL:
1845.—CAVE JOHNSON, Tennessee.
ATTORNEYS-GENERAL:
1845.—JOHN Y. MASON, Virginia.
1846.—NATHAN CLIFFORD, Maine.
1848.—ISAAC TOUCEY, Connecticut.

CONTEMPORANEOUS ENGLISH HISTORY.

Reign.—Victoria.
Premier.—Sir Robert Peel, to 1846.
Lord John Russell, to 1849 (and 1852).
Lord Lyndhurst, Lord Chancellor, fourth term since 1827.
Grant to Maynooth College. T. B. Macaulay's vote costs him his seat in the cabinet.
Failure of the Irish potato-crop, 1845. Irish famine for nearly three years.
Bright and Cobden, leaders of the Corn-law League.
Commercial and railway failures in 1847. Monetary crisis.
French Revolution, February, 1848. Riot at Glasgow, March 6.
Chartist meeting on Kennington Common, April 10.
Irish insurrection under Smith O'Brien.
Lord Palmerston's foreign policy attacked by Disraeli and Lord Stanley.
Mr. Disraeli, leader of the Protectionist party.
Numerous revolutions in Europe.
Louis Napoleon elected President of the French Republic, December, 1848.

JAMES K. POLK.

FROM — 1845 to 1849.

DURATION. — One term, — four years.

PARTY. — Democratic.

PRINCIPAL EVENTS. — War with Mexico on account of the annexation of Texas (ceded to Spain in 1819). Gen. Taylor moves to the Rio Grande; overcomes Gen. Arista at Palo Alto, Resaca de la Palma, and Matamoras. Monterey surrenders. Gen. Wool leads the army against Chihuahua. Saltillo and Tampico taken. Gen. Scott enters Vera Cruz. Retreat of Santa Anna from Buena Vista, notwithstanding his force of twenty-five thousand strong against five thousand under Taylor, Worth, Wool, Quitman, Butler, &c. Gen. Kearny enters Santa Fé, the capital of New Mexico. Capt. John C. Frémont, near San Francisco, on his Oregon exploring-expedition, hearing of the war, raises the American flag, July 5, 1846, and declares the independence of that Territory. Coms. Sloat and Stockton, two days after, assert the independence of Monterey. Com. Stockton and Capt. Frémont at once co-operate, and conquer Upper California. Expedition against Chihuahua, under Col. Doniphan, at the Sacramento Pass, Feb. 28, 1847. Gen. Scott and Com. Perry capture Vera Cruz; and the Castle of San Juan de Ulloa surrenders, March 29, 1847. On his march towards the city of Mexico, Gen. Scott meets Santa Anna at Cerro Gordo, and again defeats him. Puebla falls, also Contreras and Churubusco. Gen. Worth assaults Molino del Rey, and takes it; also the Castle of Chapultepec, the last stronghold of the capital; and Sept. 14, 1847, the American army enters the city of Mexico. Treaty closed at Guadalupe Hidalgo. Peace proclaimed by Pres. Polk, July 4, 1848. Mexico is promised fifteen million dollars, and her debts to American citizens of three millions. Cause of the war charged on Calhoun by Benton; the former having been a member of Monroe's cabinet, as Secretary of War, in 1819, "when Texas was given away." Oregon question settled with England, 1846. "The Globe," published at Washington, superseded as the administration organ, and "The Daily Union" substituted. Benton says, "It was paid for out of public money by a treasury order for fifty thousand dollars." Florida, Iowa, and Wisconsin admitted, as well as Texas. Vast gold-discoveries in California. FREESOIL PARTY organized in view of the proposed extension of slavery into California, Utah, and New Mexico. The Wilmot Proviso, "that no part of the territory to be acquired shall be open to the introduction of slavery," opposed by Mr. Calhoun's slavery resolutions, denying the right of Congress to prohibit slavery in any Territory. Great slavery agitation. Daniel Webster replies to Calhoun. Disunion proposed by South Carolina and Mississippi. Gen. Zachary Taylor elected President.

1845.—March 4. Extracts from Inaugural: "Fellow-citizens, without solicitation on my part, I have been chosen, by the free and voluntary suffrages of my countrymen, to the most honorable and most responsible office on earth. . . . With a firm reliance upon the wisdom of Omnipotence to sustain and direct me in the path of duty which I am appointed to pursue, I stand in the presence of this assembled multitude to take upon myself the solemn obligations, to the best of my ability, to preserve, protect, and defend the Constitution of the United States. . . . The government of the United States is one of delegated and limited powers; and it is by a strict adherence to the clearly-granted powers, and by abstaining from the exercise of doubtful or unauthorized implied powers, that we have the only sure guaranty against the recurrence of those unfortunate collisions between the Federal and State authorities which have occasionally so much disturbed the harmony of our system, and even threatened the perpetuity of our glorious Union. . . . Each State is a complete sovereignty within the sphere of its reserved powers. The government of the Union, acting within the sphere of its delegated authority, is also a complete sovereignty. While the General Government should abstain from the exercise of authority not clearly delegated to it, the States should be equally careful, that, in the maintenance of their rights, they do not overstep the limits of powers reserved to them. . . . The inestimable value of our Federal Union is felt and acknowledged by all. By this system of united and confederated States, our people are permitted, collectively and individually, to seek their own happiness in their own way; and the consequences have been most auspicious. Since the Union was formed, the number of the States has increased from thirteen to twenty-eight: our population has increased from three to twenty millions. New communities and States are seeking protection under its ægis, and multitudes from the Old World are flocking to our shores to participate in its blessings. Beneath its benign sway, peace and prosperity prevail. Freed from the burdens and miseries of war, our trade and intercourse have extended throughout the world. . . . Genius is free to announce its inventions and discoveries; and the hand is free to accomplish whatever the head conceives, not incompatible with the rights of a fellow-being. All distinctions of birth or of rank have been abolished. All citizens, whether native or adopted, are placed upon terms of precise equality. All are entitled to equal rights and equal protection. No union exists between

Church and State; and perfect freedom of opinion is guaranteed to all sects and creeds. . . . I am happy to believe, that, at every period of our existence as a nation, there has existed, and continues to exist, among the great mass of our people, a devotion to the union of the States, which will shield and protect it against the moral treason of any one who would seriously contemplate its destruction. . . . A national debt has become almost an institution of European monarchies. It is viewed, in some of them, as an essential prop to existing governments. Melancholy is the condition of that people whose government can be sustained only by a system which periodically transfers large amounts from the labor of the many to the coffers of the few. Such a system is incompatible with the ends for which our republican government was instituted. Under a wise policy, the debts contracted in our Revolution, and during the war of 1812, have been happily extinguished. . . . In levying a tariff of duties for the support of government, the raising of *revenue* should be the *object,* and *protection* the *incident.* . . . It is confidently believed that our system of annexation may be safely extended to the utmost bounds of our territorial limits; and that, as it shall be extended, the bonds of our Union, so far from being weakened, will become stronger. . . . I enter upon the discharge of the high duties which have been assigned me by the people, again humbly supplicating that Divine Being, who has watched over and protected our beloved country from its infancy to the present hour, to continue his gracious benedictions upon us, that we may continue to be a prosperous and happy people.

" JAMES K. POLK."

ADMINISTRATIONS

OF

ZACHARY TAYLOR AND MILLARD FILLMORE.

1849 TO 1853.

THE CABINET.

PRESIDENTS:
ZACHARY TAYLOR, LOUISIANA,
(Died July 9, 1850.)
MILLARD FILLMORE, NEW YORK.

VICE-PRESIDENT:
MILLARD FILLMORE, NEW YORK.

SECRETARIES OF STATE:
1849.— JOHN M. CLAYTON, Delaware.
1850.— DANIEL WEBSTER, Massachusetts.
1852.— EDWARD EVERETT, Massachusetts.

SECRETARIES OF THE TREASURY:
1849.— WILLIAM M. MEREDITH, Pennsylvania.
1850.— THOMAS CORWIN, Ohio.

SECRETARIES OF WAR:
1849.— GEORGE W. CRAWFORD, Georgia.
1850.— CHARLES M. CONRAD, Louisiana.

SECRETARIES OF THE NAVY:
1849.— WILLIAM B. PRESTON, Virginia.
1850.— WILLIAM A. GRAHAM, North Carolina.
1852.— JOHN P. KENNEDY, Maryland.

SECRETARIES OF THE INTERIOR:
1849.— THOMAS EWING, Ohio.
1850.— ALEXANDER H. H. STUART, Virginia.

POSTMASTERS-GENERAL:
1849.— JACOB COLLAMER, Vermont.
1850.— NATHAN K. HALL, New York.
1852.— SAMUEL D. HUBBARD, Connecticut.

ATTORNEYS-GENERAL:
1849.— REVERDY JOHNSON, Maryland.
1850.— JOHN J. CRITTENDEN, Kentucky.

CONTEMPORANEOUS ENGLISH HISTORY.
Reign.— Victoria.
Premier.— Lord John Russell; resigned Feb. 22, 1851.
From Feb. 22 to March 3 there was virtually no administration. Duke of Wellington, Queen's counsellor.
Earl of Derby, February to December, 1852.
Earl of Aberdeen, 1852 to 1853 (and 1855).
Sir Robert Peel died July 2, 1850, in consequence of a fall from his horse.
Burmese War commenced October, 1851.
Coup d'État in Paris, Dec. 2, 1851. Louis Napoleon, President; recognized as Emperor, Dec. 6, 1852.
The Duke of Wellington died Sept. 14, 1852.

ZACHARY TAYLOR AND MILLARD FILLMORE.

FROM — 1849 to 1853.

DURATION. — One term, — four years.

PARTY. — Whig.

PRINCIPAL EVENTS. — Great slavery agitation. Discussions between Calhoun and Webster. Southern leaders determined to carry slaves into Texas and other new territory. Calhoun draws up a Southern manifesto for the dissolution of the Union, and obtains forty-two signatures to it. Secession conventions are held in South Carolina and Mississippi. Pres. Taylor stands by the Union. Southerners oppose the admission of California as a free State. Henry Clay, a member of the House in 1821 (Monroe's administration), and author of the Missouri Compromise of that year, proposes a consolidation of all past compromises on the slavery question into one bill of thirty-nine sections, called "The Omnibus Bill of 1850." After eight months' heated discussion, the bill, powerfully opposed by Benton on account of its embracing so many subjects, is lost; and the States and Territories are admitted by separate acts, as follows: —

Utah Territory Bill, Aug. 10, 1850.

Texas Boundary Bill, Aug. 10, 1850.

California State Bill, Aug. 13, 1850.

New-Mexico Territory Bill, Aug. 14, 1850.

Fugitive-slave Bill, Aug. 23, 1850.

Abolition of slave-trade in District of Columbia, Sept. 14, 1850.

In the course of the discussion, Jefferson Davis requires that the Missouri line of compromise to New Mexico and California shall be extended to the Pacific, with the right to hold slaves in new territory below the line. Calhoun in his last address, read by Mr. Mason, after alluding to the antislavery ordinance of 1787 (no more slavery in the North-west) and the Missouri compromises of 1820-1821, admits that the first agitation for the dissolution of the Union commenced in 1835. Daniel Webster delivers a conciliatory speech, March 7, 1850. Death of John C. Calhoun, March 31, 1850: he graduated at Yale College in 1804 with high honors: his father, Patrick Calhoun, was born in Ireland. Death of Pres. Taylor, July 9, 1850: "*The nation mourns his loss.*" Millard Fillmore is inaugurated President, July 10, 1850; Daniel Webster, Secretary of State. Upon the passage of the California Bill, ten Southern senators offer a protest. Robert C. Winthrop raises the question of reception of protest, to keep it from the journal of the Senate; and the bill is duly sent to the House, and passed. John C. Frémont and William M. Gwinn of California take their seats as senators. Fugitive-slave Law terribly obnoxious. Mormon trouble increasing. Webster and Hulsemann correspondence. Gen. Lopez, a Spaniard, attempts a revolution in Cuba. Search is made for Sir John Franklin by the Grinnell and United-States expeditions, under Dr. Kane. Spain, France, and England join in a "tripartite treaty" not to take Cuba. Death of Henry Clay and Daniel Webster in 1852. Election of Charles Sumner to the Senate of 1852, and Nathaniel P. Banks to the House of 1854. Mrs. Beecher Stowe's "Uncle Tom's Cabin," published in 1851, enters upon its world-wide mission. Kossuth visits the United States, and obtains $100,000 for Hungary. The Whig party, by compromises with slavery, is destroyed; and Franklin Pierce of New Hampshire is elected President, and William Rufus King of Alabama Vice-President, to March 4, 1857.

1849. — Extract from the first and only Annual Message of Pres. Taylor: "Attachment to the Union of the States should be habitually fostered in every American heart. For more than half a century, during which kingdoms and empires have fallen, this Union has stood unshaken. The patriots who formed it have long since descended to the grave; yet still it remains the proudest monument to their memory, and the object of affection and admiration with every one worthy to bear the American name. . . . Upon its preservation must depend our own happiness and that of countless generations to come. Whatever dangers may threaten it, I shall stand by it, and maintain it in its integrity to the full extent of the obligations imposed and the power conferred upon me by the Constitution. . . . .

"ZACHARY TAYLOR."

PIERCE'S ADMINISTRATION.

1853 TO 1857.

THE CABINET.

PRESIDENT:
FRANKLIN PIERCE, New Hampshire.

VICE-PRESIDENT:
WILLIAM R. KING, Alabama (died 1853).

SECRETARY OF STATE:
1853. — William L. Marcy, New York.

SECRETARY OF THE TREASURY:
1853. — James Guthrie, Kentucky.

SECRETARY OF WAR:
1853. — Jefferson Davis, Mississippi.

SECRETARY OF THE NAVY:
1853. — James C. Dobbin, North Carolina.

SECRETARY OF THE INTERIOR:
1853. — Robert McClelland, Michigan.

POSTMASTER-GENERAL:
1853. — James Campbell, Pennsylvania.

ATTORNEY-GENERAL:
1853. — Caleb Cushing, Massachusetts.

CONTEMPORANEOUS ENGLISH HISTORY.

Reign. — Victoria.
Premier. — Earl of Aberdeen, to 1855.
Lord Palmerston, to 1857 (and 1858).
Dispute between Russia and Turkey.
War with Russia declared March 27, 1854.
(Crimea, Alma, Balaklava, Inkermann, Sebastopol.)
Treaty of peace signed at Paris, March 30, 1856.
English loss, 24,000 men.
French loss, 63,500 men.
Russian loss, 500,000 men.
English debt and taxes increased eighty-two million pounds sterling.
War between England and Persia, November to March, 1857.

FRANKLIN PIERCE.

FROM — 1853 to 1857.
DURATION. — One term, — four years.
PARTY. — Democratic.
PRINCIPAL EVENTS. — Death of Vice-President W. R. King, April 18, 1853. Dispute, under the treaty of Guadalupe Hidalgo, respecting boundary-lines in New Mexico. Mesilla-valley road to California purchased by the United States of Santa Anna, President of the Republic of Mexico, for ten million dollars. Isthmus of Tehuantepec Railroad arranged for. Free navigation of the Gulf of California and River Colorado included in the purchase. Treaty concluded with Japan. Two ports opened to the United States by Com. Perry. Dr. Kane's second search for Sir John Franklin. Expeditions over the Rocky Mountains to the Pacific. Railway route surveyed. Koszta, the Hungarian refugee at Smyrna, is rescued as an American citizen by Capt. Ingraham. Senator Stephen A. Douglas of Illinois, in 1854, advocates the Kansas-Nebraska Bill; the people of those vast territories to decide for themselves the question of slavery. Messrs. Everett, Sumner, Wade, Houston, and Bell, oppose it. By the Missouri compromises of 1820-1821, slavery being excluded from this region, the free States insist that it shall be *forever* excluded. A bill making void the Missouri Compromise, after a long and bitter contest, is passed, and signed by the President, May, 1854. Emigration to Kansas swiftly follows. "Squatter sovereignty" is established. Quarrels ensue. The polls are managed by armed men from the South. Free-States men hold conventions, and are

finally successful in forming and adopting a State government: but outrages are numberless, resulting in civil war in that territory; and their representative to Washington is rejected. Nathaniel P. Banks, after an exciting contest, is elected speaker of the Thirty-fourth Congress. In 1855, Henry Wilson succeeds Edward Everett in the Senate. In 1856, Anson Burlingame succeeds William Appleton in the House. May 2, 1856, Charles Sumner is brutally assaulted in the Capitol by Brooks of South Carolina for words spoken in debate. The entire country is again aroused. William Lloyd Garrison favors the Republican party. Rev. Henry Ward Beecher recommends Sharp's rifles, as well as Bibles, for Kansas. The American party asserts that "Americans shall rule America." The three candidates for the Presidency are James Buchanan, Democrat; John C. Frémont, Republican; Ex-President Millard Fillmore, American. James Buchanan is elected.

1856.—Extract from the Annual Message of Pres. Pierce: "Extremes beget extremes. Violent attack from the North finds its inevitable consequence in the growth of a spirit of angry defiance at the South. Thus, in the progress of events, we have reached that consummation,—which the voice of the people has now so pointedly rebuked,—of the attempt of a portion of the States, by a sectional organization and movement, to usurp the control of the government of the United States. . . .

"FRANKLIN PIERCE."

BUCHANAN'S ADMINISTRATION.

1857 TO 1861.

THE CABINET.

PRESIDENT:
JAMES BUCHANAN, PENNSYLVANIA.

VICE-PRESIDENT:
JOHN C. BRECKINRIDGE, KENTUCKY.

SECRETARIES OF STATE:
1857. — LEWIS CASS, Michigan.
1860. — JEREMIAH S. BLACK, Pennsylvania.

SECRETARIES OF THE TREASURY:
1857. — HOWELL COBB, Georgia.
1860. — PHILIP F. THOMAS, Maryland.
1861. — JOHN A. DIX, New York.

SECRETARIES OF WAR:
1857. — JOHN B. FLOYD, Virginia.
1861. — JOSEPH HOLT, Kentucky.

SECRETARY OF THE NAVY:
1857. — ISAAC TOUCEY, Connecticut.

SECRETARY OF THE INTERIOR
1857. — JACOB THOMPSON, Mississippi.

POSTMASTERS-GENERAL:
1857. — AARON V. BROWN, Tennessee.
1859. — JOSEPH HOLT, Kentucky.
1861. — HORATIO KING, Maine.

ATTORNEYS-GENERAL:
1857. — JEREMIAH S. BLACK, Pennsylvania.
1860. — EDWIN M. STANTON, Pennsylvania.

CONTEMPORANEOUS ENGLISH HISTORY.

Reign. — Victoria.
Premier. — Lord Palmerston, to 1858. Earl of Derby, 1859. Lord Palmerston, 1861.
Indian Mutiny. Chinese War. Reform Bill.
Commercial crisis, 1857. Religious revival.
After a struggle of eight years, Lord John Russell obtains a bill enabling Jews to sit in Parliament; and Baron Rothschild is admitted July 26, 1858
France and Austria at war from May to July, 1859, about Austrian dominion in Piedmont.
Cotton famine on account of the Rebellion in America.

JAMES BUCHANAN.

FROM — March 4, 1857, to 1861.
DURATION. — One term, — four years.
PARTY. — Democratic.
PRINCIPAL EVENTS. — Chief Justice Taney decides, in the Dred Scott case, that the Missouri Compromise is unconstitutional. The proslavery and antislavery parties, the former re-asserting that "slavery is a divinely-appointed institution," are again intensely agitated. Personal-liberty laws are passed in the free States to counteract the operation of the Fugitive-slave Law. Kansas-Nebraska matters continue vexatious beyond expression. Entire families with Northern sentiments are massacred; and party-disputes are settled by the pistol and bowie-knife. John Brown and twenty associates, driven to desperation, on the night of Oct. 16, 1859, rashly seize the United-States arsenal at Harper's Ferry, Va., with a view to obtaining arms to liberate slaves. They are overpowered by Col. Robert E. Lee; thirteen being killed during the affray; two escape; and six, including their leader, are tried, condemned, and executed in Charleston, Va. Added to these distresses, commercial and financial disasters visit the great mercantile centres of the country, commencing in 1857, producing a wonderful revival of religion in New York and elsewhere. The Fulton-street "Business-Men's Noonday Prayer-Meeting" is organized during the crisis. New political questions are raised, resulting in the nomination of four distinct party-candidates for the Presidency. The Republicans nominate Abraham Lincoln of Illinois. The Democrats have

two candidates; viz., Stephen A. Douglas of Illinois, and John C. Breckinridge of Kentucky. The *Union party* nominate John Bell of Tennessee. Upon the election of Abraham Lincoln, in the autumn of 1860, South Carolina. Mississippi, Florida, Alabama, Georgia, Louisiana, and Texas join in secession from the Union; and, a few months later, Virginia, Arkansas, Tennessee, and North Carolina, follow them. The first six combined form a confederacy of the South at Montgomery, Ala., Feb. 8, 1861, called the *Confederate States of America;* elect Jefferson Davis of Mississippi, President; Alexander H. Stephens of Georgia, Vice-President; and, before Lincoln is inaugurated President of the United States, commence war upon the Federal Government, seizing treasury-funds, munitions of war, custom-houses, ships. and forts, and robbing the country generally. "Sedition, privy conspiracy, and rebellion" rule in the South; and "confusion worse confounded" reigns at Washington. Treason is suspected everywhere; the majority of the Buchanan cabinet resign; Southern members leave their seats in Congress; and, on his way to the capital, Abraham Lincoln, the President-elect, is obliged to be attended by a body-guard. Meantime, in January, 1861, the steamship "Star of the West," unarmed, on her way with troops and provisions to Fort Sumter, in Charleston (South Carolina) harbor, is fired upon by a rebel battery, and forced to return to New York. But Lincoln is finally inaugurated President. Minnesota is admitted in 1858; Oregon, in 1859; and, after a four-years' war, Kansas, in 1861.

1857.—Extracts from the Inaugural Address: "I feel a humble confidence that the kind Providence which inspired our fathers with wisdom to frame the most perfect form of government and union ever devised by man will not suffer it to perish until it shall have been peacefully instrumental, by its example, in the extension of civil and religious liberty throughout the world. . . . Our present financial condition is without a parallel in history. No nation has ever before been embarrassed from too large a surplus in its treasury. . . . It is our glory, that, while other nations have extended their dominions by the sword, we have never acquired any territory except by fair purchase, or, as in the case of Texas, by the voluntary determination of a brave, kindred, and independent people to blend their destinies with our own. Even our acquisitions from Mexico form no exception. Unwilling to take advantage of the fortune of war against a sister republic, we purchased these possessions, under the treaty of peace, for a sum which was considered at the time a fair equivalent. . . . Acting on this principle, no nation will have a right to interfere or to complain, if, in the progress of events, we shall still further extend our possessions. . . .   "JAMES BUCHANAN."

ADMINISTRATIONS

OF

ABRAHAM LINCOLN AND ANDREW JOHNSON.

1861 TO 1869.

THE CABINET.

PRESIDENTS:
1861.—ABRAHAM LINCOLN, Illinois.
1865.—ANDREW JOHNSON, Tennessee.

VICE-PRESIDENTS:
1861.—HANNIBAL HAMLIN, Maine.
1865.—ANDREW JOHNSON, Tennessee.

SECRETARY OF STATE:
1861.—William H. Seward, New York.

SECRETARIES OF THE TREASURY:
1861.—Salmon P. Chase, Ohio.
1864.—William Pitt Fessenden, Maine.
1865.—Hugh McCulloch, Indiana.

SECRETARIES OF WAR:
1861.—Simon Cameron, Pennsylvania.
1861.—Edwin M. Stanton, Pennsylvania.
1867.—Ulysses S. Grant, Illinois.
1868.—John M. Schofield, Missouri.

SECRETARY OF THE NAVY:
1861.—Gideon Welles, Connecticut.

SECRETARIES OF THE INTERIOR:
1861.—Caleb B. Smith, Indiana.
1863.—John P. Usher, Indiana.
1865.—James Harlan, Iowa.
1866.—O. H. Browning, Illinois.

POSTMASTERS-GENERAL:
1861.—Montgomery Blair, Maryland.
1864.—William Denison, Ohio.
1866.—A. W. Randall, Wisconsin.

ATTORNEYS-GENERAL:
1861.—Edward Bates, Missouri.
1864.—James J Speed, Kentucky.
1866.—Henry Stanberry, Ohio.
1868.—William M. Evarts, New York.

CONTEMPORANEOUS ENGLISH HISTORY.

Reign.—Victoria
Premier — Lord Palmerston, to 1865. Earl Russell, to 1866. Earl of Derby (3d time), to 1868. Mr. Disraeli and Mr. Gladstone, 1869.
Death of the Prince Consort, Dec. 14, 1861.
Prince of Wales marries Alexandra of Denmark, March 10, 1863.
Death of Mr. Cobden, April 2, 1865. Murder of Pres. Lincoln announced. Unanimous addresses, expressive of sorrow and indignation, passed in both Houses of Parliament. Death of Lord Palmerston, at eighty-one, Oct. 18. Fenian conspiracy in Ireland.
Reform debates. Abyssinian War. Debates on the Irish Church. Liberal party united under Mr. Gladstone. Disestablishment of the Irish Church. Death of Lord Derby, Oct. 23, 1869.

ABRAHAM LINCOLN.

FROM — March 4, 1861, to 1869.

DURATION. — Two terms, — eight years.

PARTY. — Republican.

PRINCIPAL EVENTS. — Pres. Lincoln is inaugurated March 4, 1861. Gen. Scott has six hundred troops under his command at Washington; but the inauguration proceeds without difficulty. Fort Sumter is bombarded, April 12 and 13, by Gen. Beauregard; and surrenders Sunday, P.M., April 14. The President's proclamation for seventy-five thousand militia of the Union to serve three months under Gen. Scott is issued April 15. Senator Wilson telegraphs to Gov. Andrew, who at once responds to the call. At sundown, four regiments of Massachusetts troops are assembled in Boston, and "the day following," says Lossing, "are on Boston Common, mustered in regular order, with banners flying, and bayonets gleaming; each company with full ranks." Five Pennsylvania companies, without arms, reach Washington at night, April 17, and, quartered in the Capitol, are warmly welcomed by the administration of the United States, and members of the Washington Young Men's Christian Association. April 17, the day on which Jefferson Davis issues Montgomery letters of marque and reprisal to interfere with commerce, the Sixth Regiment of Massachusetts Volunteers leaves Boston for Washington. April 19, the anniversary of the battle at Lexington (April 19, 1775), they are attacked in the streets of Baltimore: three men are killed outright, and one is mortally wounded. The troops reach Washington on the evening of the 19th, and are the first full regiment who have answered the call. Moses H. Grinnell of New York and Judge Crosby of Lowell, almost simultaneously and without conference, under date of April 17 and 18, issue personal relief subscription-papers for the soldiers and their families, and give a hundred dollars each towards the fund: and " the women of Bridgeport, Conn.," says Goodrich, " met together to roll bandages and prepare lint as early as April 15; and on the same day Miss Almena B. Bates of Charlestown, Mass., suggested similar philanthropic work." The Soldiers' Aid Society is organized in New York, April 20; also one in Cleveland, O., on the same day. "April 21, the ladies of Dr. Taylor's church, Philadelphia, organize a society, and make arrangements" (says the Rev. Mr. Moss) "for the preparation of bedding, bandages, lint, &c." And from this and kindred Ladies' Aid Societies originate the "United-States Christian Commission," led by George H. Stuart of Philadelphia, Edward S. Tobey and Charles Demond of Boston, and J. V. Farwell of Chicago, and the "United-States Sanitary Commission," led by the Rev. Dr. Bellows of New York. Miss D. L. Dix, witnessing the mob at Baltimore, accompanies the Sixth Regiment to Washington, and offers her services in the welfare of the sick. Acting Surgeon Gen. R. C. Wood " cheerfully and thankfully accepts them." Representatives from the Christian Associations of the country, and others in all the regiments, are constantly visited by friends with food, garments, and thousands of dollars from home through the two great Commissions; who also furnish them with Bibles, Testaments, and tracts in large numbers. Placards, "Sumter on Fire," " Rebels firing on the Burning Fort," and other hourly announcements, excite the freemen of the Republic to the highest enthusiasm; and, within two weeks from the date of the President's proclamation, upwards of three hundred thousand men offer their services in the defence of the Union. April 18, the arsenal at Harper's Ferry is seized by Virginia troops; April 21, the navy-yard at Norfolk. May 16, Ex-Gov. N. P. Banks,

Benjamin F. Butler, and John A. Dix, are commissioned major-generals by Pres. Lincoln. George B. McClellan's and John C. Frémont's commissions are dated May 14. Major Anderson is made a brigadier-general. Richmond becomes the rebel capital. The first meeting of the Confederate Congress occurs July 20. Meantime, in April, as preparations are being made to secure and repair the frigate " Pennsylvania," the " Columbus," " Delaware," " New York," " United States," " Columbia," " Raritan," " Plymouth," " Germantown," " Dolphin," and " Merrimack," at Gosport Navy-Yard, opposite Norfolk, the entire fleet, through the treachery of professed loyalists, apparently falling into the hands of secessionists, an order is given by Com. McCauley to scuttle and sink ship by ship. Capt. (afterwards Admiral) Paulding arrives from Washington just as the work is being accomplished, and orders that the ships and navy-yard shall be fired. Notwithstanding the immense conflagration, destroying millions of property, only a portion of the vessels and navy-yard are burned; and the measure proves in many respects a failure. The next movement of the enemy is an attempt to capture Washington, and proclaim Jefferson Davis dictator. Butler and his troops save the frigate " Constitution." Baltimore is under the control of secessionists. Pres. Lincoln says, " I must have troops for the defence of the capital. The Carolinians are now marching across Virginia to seize the capital, and hang me. What am I to do? I must have troops, I say; and as they can neither crawl under Maryland, nor fly over it, they must come across it." Twigg's treason in Texas having greatly reduced the regular army, the question is agitated respecting a call for volunteers as well as militia. Col. Robert E. Lee of Arlington is promised the position of general-in-chief of the Confederate forces, and tenders his resignation as an officer of the United States. Officers, both army and navy, are proving traitors; and the city of Washington is not only threatened with capture, but conflagration. For several days, the President and cabinet are surrounded by a body-guard in the Capitol. The basement of the building is subsequently turned into an immense bakery, with arrangements for regular army-rations. Within ten days from the first proclamation and call for troops, eight thousand men, well armed, from New York, under direction of Gen. John E. Wool and the Union Defence Committee, arrive at Washington; and the capital is saved from seizure. Col. Frank E. Howe voluntarily receives, and handsomely entertains at his warehouse, New-England soldiers on their way through New York. May 4, a Union meeting is held at Baltimore; and the army passing through the city is under the protection of Gen. Butler at the Relay House. He afterwards, May 14, occupies the city, and forbids the display of secession flags, &c. Washington City being well garrisoned, Arlington Heights and Alexandria are occupied by Federal troops; and Gen. Butler takes command at Fortress Monroe, and declares escaped slaves "contraband of war." Major Theodore Winthrop of Butler's staff, who fell at Big Bethel a few days later, wrote, "An epigram abolished slavery in the United States." Commissioners of the Confederacy, so called, are now on their way to Europe to enlist the sympathy, aid, and recognition of foreign powers. Jefferson Davis's authorized pirates watch the commerce of the United States; and "insurrection becomes rebellion." June 10, an unsuccessful attack is made by Union troops under Butler at Big Bethel and Newport News. June 27, Gen. Banks issues his Baltimore proclamation, and arrests the marshal of police. In July, Gen. McDowell moves with Union troops to Manassas Junction, and meets Gen. Beauregard of the Southern army. The first battle of Bull Run is fought Sunday, July 21; and the Union troops, by the sudden and unexpected appearance of Johnston's army of the Shenandoah, are panic-stricken, and driven back to Washington. This is the first great battle of the Rebellion. Congress appropriates five hundred million dollars to carry on the war, and authorizes the President to call for five hundred thousand men; and Gen. George B. McClellan is called to the command of the Army of the Potomac. Months are spent in organizing and disciplining the army. The battle at Ball's Bluff is fought in October; and Union troops are again defeated. Col. (Senator) Baker of Oregon is killed. McClellan succeeds Lieut.-Gen. Winfield Scott, who retires from service by the infirmities of age, Nov. 1, 1861.

[Although this is not a *handbook of the naval and military operations of the United States*, we shall give details of battles from various histories, as far as space will permit.]

1861. — Turning from the eastern to the western section of the country, we find, that commencing with the nomination of Lincoln, whose home is Springfield, Ill., thousands of liberty-loving people are educating themselves for the impending crisis; and, upon the surrender of Sumter, tens of thousands, afterwards hundreds of thousands, are preparing to move for the protection of Washington and the Republic. As early as Jan. 12, the Legislature of Ohio passes a series of resolutions denouncing the secession movement. In April, George B. McClellan, Superintendent of the Ohio and Mississippi Railroad, is commissioned a major-general of all the forces of that State; and Camp Dennison is established. In March, Gov. Morton of Indiana is preparing for action; and, finally, two hundred thousand troops are sent to the war. Gov. Yates of Illinois calls for an extra session of the legislature, April 23; and thousands of men are at once at Cairo and the confluence of the Ohio and the Mississippi Rivers. Stephen A. Douglas denounces treason, and works for the Union like a true patriot; but, on the 3d of June, he is removed from earthly labors. Millions of money, and thousands of troops, are freely offered by the legislatures of the above States, and Michigan, Wisconsin, Iowa, Minnesota, and others combined? Western Virginia is truly loyal; but Missouri and Kentucky are *temporarily* wanting. Returning to the Potomac, we find Ellsworth's Zouaves at Alexandria May 23. Their noble commander is shot dead by Jackson of the Marshall House. Again the country is determined to put down treason. A regiment is formed in New York, called "Ellsworth's Avengers." Dr. Russell, correspondent of "The London Times," constantly predicts the success of the rebels. The great agitation of the day is to capture Richmond; and "Forward to Richmond!" is the war-cry. Col. Duryéa of New York is assigned the command of Camp Hamilton. June 4, the position is given to Brig.-Gen. Price of Massachusetts. Magruder abandons his flag, and becomes a Confederate general: this, too, after he had said to President Lincoln, "Every one else may desert you; but *I* never will." Gen. Butler leaves Fortress Monroe Aug. 18. Col. Wallace is victorious in North-Western Virginia. Rosecrans succeeds McClellan in the Shenandoah, July, 1861, at Beverly and Rich Mountain, and continues successful attempts to clear West Virginia of rebels. McClellan conducts a rout at Carrick's Ford. Turning again westward, we find Missouri and Kentucky divided in council. Gov. Jackson of Missouri is a persistent rebel; while a majority of the citizens are loyal. Gen. John Pope is in North Missouri. Capt. Lyon holds the arsenal for the Union, captures Confederate troops, and puts the governor to flight. A battle is fought on Wilson's Creek, Aug. 10; and Gen. Lyon is killed. Another disastrous battle is fought in September. Gen. Frémont, commander of the Western Department, takes the field in person, proclaims martial law, and declares the slaves of rebels free; but soon after, in November, turns over the command to Gen. Hunter. Subsequently, Gen. Henry W. Halleck is appointed to the same department. In November, Gen. Ulysses S. Grant, with three thousand men, goes down the river from Cairo, and attacks Belmont, Mo.: they are obliged to return to Cairo. Kentucky is, by majority, loyal to the Union; but secessionists keep her neutral. In September, rebel Gen. Polk invades the State, and seizes Columbus. Gen. Grant, entering, takes possession of Paducah; and Kentucky soon decides for the Union. The Confederates concentrate at Bowling Green; but Federal armies drive them southward. The naval and military expeditions of 1861 are under the command of Commodore Stringham, Gen. Butler, Commodore Dupont, and Gen. T. W. Sherman. The first, in August, captures Hatteras Inlet, N.C.; and the second, Port Royal, S.C. By these and other means, the entire Southern coast is completely blockaded. The principal Confederate cruiser of the year is the steamer "Sumter," Capt. Semmes. She is left at Gibraltar; her officers proceeding to England for a better steamship ("The Alabama"). Both England and France recognize the Confederacy as a belligerent power, an established government; and, in the "Trent" affair, England threatens war against the United States unless Ex-Senators Mason and Slidell (Confederate commissioners taken by Capt. Wilkes and Lieut. Fairfax of "The San Jacinto" from the British steamer "Trent," near Cuba, Nov. 8, and sent to Fort Warren, Boston harbor) are handed over to the British Government. Although British precedents are all in favor of retaining them (and the ship too), Pres. Lincoln, who from the first regretted the capture, says with Sumner, "Let them go;" and they are duly liberated Russia stands by the Union.

1862. — The strength of the United-States army, Jan. 1, 1862, is five hundred and seventy-five thousand men, — two hundred thousand at Washington, under McClellan; two hundred thousand in Kentucky, under Grant, Halleck, and Buell; a hundred and seventy-five thousand scattered throughout South Carolina, Fortress Monroe, the Lower Potomac, the Upper Potomac, Western Virginia, &c., under Gens. Sherman, Wool, Banks, Hooker, Kelley, and Rosecrans. The strength of the Confederate Army is about three hundred and fifty thousand, increased by conscription. During the year, slavery is prohibited in the Territories of the United States and the District of Columbia. Colored troops are enlisted in the army, and a "test oath" is demanded. A few troops are raised by draft.

Jan. 19.—A victory is gained by Federal troops, under Gen. George H. Thomas, at Mill Spring, on the Mississippi.

Feb. 6.—Fort Henry, on the Tennessee, captured by Com. Foote.

Feb. 16.—Fort Donelson, on the Cumberland, bombarded three days, surrenders to Grant. Sixteen thousand prisoners taken.

Bowling Green and Columbus are evacuated.

Nashville, Tenn., is occupied by Federal Gen. Nelson.

Andrew Johnson is appointed military governor of Tennessee.

Gen. Grant, with forty thousand men, meets Gens. Albert Sydney Johnston and Beauregard, who also have forty thousand; and a a desperate battle is fought at Shiloh, the Confederates retreating to Corinth, Miss.

Two French princes of the House of Orleans, the *Comte de Paris* and the *Duc de Chartres*, visiting the capital with their uncle the Prince de Joinville, son of the late Louis Philippe, King of the French, are staff-officers under Gen. McClellan from November, 1861, to July, 1862.

In July, Gen. Halleck is appointed commander-in-chief of the Federal army.

Confederate Gens. Van Dorn and Price attempt the capture of Corinth, held by Grant and Rosecrans. They are unsuccessful, and lose more than ten thousand men. Union loss about three thousand.

Gen. Buell opposes Bragg in East Tennessee, and holds Nashville and Louisville, Ky.

Gen. Kirby Smith enters Lexington, and in September threatens Cincinnati, O.

Guerillas, under Morgan and Forrest, are scattered throughout Kentucky, Tennessee, and Indiana. Soon after the defeat at Cumberland Gap, Gen. Buell is superseded by Gen. Rosecrans, who gains a victory over Bragg, near Murfreesborough, Dec. 31.

West of the Mississippi, the Federals, under Sigel, are victorious at Pea Ridge in March, 1862.

April 7.—Island No. 10, after three weeks' cannonading, surrenders to Gen. Pope and Com. Foote; and Pope returns to Corinth.

Memphis falls, and the Mississippi is open to Vicksburg.

Gens. Grant and William T. Sherman make an unsuccessful attack on Vicksburg; one of the Federal garrisons having disgracefully surrendered. Admiral Farragut, with his fleet, runs the gantlet of the forts below New Orleans. Rear-Admiral Porter captures that city. B. F. Butler takes military possession, and confiscates the property of the disloyal. The fleet and admirals, proceeding up the river, capture Baton Rouge and Natchez, encounter the rebel ram "Arkansas," pass the batteries at Vicksburg, and join the Union fleet above. Gen. Banks succeeds Gen. Butler at New Orleans. Pensacola, Fla., is evacuated May 9; Galveston in October, afterwards recaptured by Texans. The Port-Royal expedition captures Fernandina and other Florida ports; and Fort Pulaski surrenders to Gen. Hunter, who issues a proclamation of freedom.

Early in 1862, Gen. Burnside and Com. Goldsborough set sail from Fortress Monroe for Roanoke Island, which is duly taken, also other places on the North-Carolina coast; Newbern, March 14; Beaufort on the 25th; Fort Macon, April 25. The memorable fight between the rebel ram "Merrimack" and Ericsson's little "Monitor" occurs in Hampton Road March 8. "The Merrimack" is driven back to Norfolk, and the Union fleet is saved.

In Virginia, February, 1862, Gen. Lander is successful on the Potomac; and Gen. N. P. Banks drives Stonewall Jackson up the Valley of the Shenandoah. Gen. Shields wins at Winchester. McClellan takes possession of Manassas March 10, and on the 11th is relieved as general-in-chief, and conducts the Army of the Potomac.

Gen. Frémont takes command of troops in West Virginia and Tennessee; Gen. Banks, of those in the Shenandoah; and Gen. McDowell, of those on the Rappahannock. McClellan, with a hundred thousand men, commences his Peninsular campaign towards Richmond via Alexandria, Fortress Monroe, the James and York Rivers. Yorktown is evacuated; also Williamsburg. Gen. Wool takes possession of Norfolk in May. Union gunboats repulsed at Fort Darling. McClellan reaches White House on the Pamunkey, and holds Chickahominy, near Seven Pines and Fair Oaks. Rebel Gen. Johnston, being wounded, is relieved by Robert E. Lee, who becomes Richmond's defender. Gen. McClellan relies upon re-enforcements from McDowell's army, near Fredericksburg; and Gen. Fitz John Porter is stationed at Hanover Court House. Stonewall Jackson, re-enforced to twenty thousand men, is ordered to attack the army under Gen. Banks, at Strasburg, of less than six thousand. Washington is threatened, and McDowell is compelled to return. Jackson joins Lee before Richmond; and another month is lost by McClellan, who transfers his army to the banks of the James. The Confederates are repulsed at Malvern Hill, July 1, after several terrible battles known as "Seven Days before Richmond." McClellan holds Harrison's Landing, and Lee returns to the rebel capital. The Army of Virginia is placed under Gen. Pope. Frémont resigns. In July, Gen. Halleck becomes general-in-chief of the Union army. Lee commences operations against Pope at Cedar Mountain, Aug. 9. Pope moves to the Rapidan, thence to the Rappahannock. On the 26th, Jackson enters Thoroughfare Gap, and cuts off Pope's railroad-connection with Washington. Gen. Hooker meets Confederate troops at Kettle Run under Gen. Ewell; and battles are fought at Manassas, Groveton, Bull Run, and Chantilly. Federal Gens. Stevens and Kearny are killed. The Union troops return to Washington. Gen. Pope resigns; and the army is placed under the command of McClellan for the defence of the capital. Gen. Lee, flushed with success, crosses the Potomac to enter Maryland. McClellan overtakes him near the Cumberland Valley, at South Mountain, and drives him across the mountain. Sept. 15, Harper's Ferry surrenders to Jackson, who immediately joins Lee at Antietam Creek and Sharpsburg. Sept. 17, the great battle of Antietam is fought, and Lee is forced to recross the Potomac. In November, McClellan surrenders his command to Gen. Burnside; and Burnside, through no fault of his, is unsuccessful in an attempt to capture Richmond by Fredericksburg. He is subsequently appointed to the command of the Department of the Ohio.

EMANCIPATION PROCLAMATION, JAN. 1, 1863.

WHEREAS, on the twenty-second day of September, in the year of our Lord one thousand eight hundred and sixty-two, a proclamation was issued by the President of the United States, containing among other things the following; to wit, "That on the first day of January, in the year of our Lord one thousand eight hundred and sixty-three, all persons held as slaves within any State, or designated part of a State, the people whereof shall then be in rebellion against the United States, shall be then, thenceforward, and forever free; and the Executive Government of the United States, including the military and naval authority thereof, will recognize and maintain the freedom of such persons, and will do no act or acts to repress such persons, or any of them, in any efforts they may make for their actual freedom; that the Executive will, on the first day of

January aforesaid, by proclamation, designate the States, and parts of States, if any, in which the people thereof, respectively, shall then be in rebellion against the United States; and the fact that any State, or the people thereof, shall on that day be in good faith represented in the Congress of the United States by members chosen thereto at elections wherein a majority of the qualified voters of such States shall have participated, shall, in the absence of strong countervailing testimony, be deemed conclusive evidence that such State, and the people thereof, are not then in rebellion against the United States:"—

Now, therefore, I, Abraham Lincoln, President of the United States, by virtue of the power in me vested as commander-in-chief of the army and navy of the United States in time of actual armed rebellion against the authority and government of the United States, and as a fit and necessary war-measure for suppressing said rebellion, do, on this first day of January, in the year of our Lord one thousand eight hundred and sixty-three, and in accordance with my purpose so to do, publicly proclaimed for the full period of one hundred days from the day first above mentioned, order and designate as the States, and parts of States, wherein the people thereof, respectively, are this day in rebellion against the United States, the following, — to wit, Arkansas, Texas, Louisiana (except the parishes of St. Bernard, Plaquemines, Jefferson, St. John, St. Charles, St. James, Ascension, Assumption, Terre-Bonne, Lafourche, Ste. Marie, St. Martin, and Orleans, including the city of New Orleans), Mississippi, Alabama, Florida, Georgia, South Carolina, North Carolina, and Virginia (except the forty-eight counties designated as West Virginia, and also the counties of Berkeley, Accomac, Northampton, Elizabeth City, York, Princess Anna, and Norfolk, including the cities of Norfolk and Portsmouth), — and which excepted parts are, for the present, left precisely as if this proclamation were not issued. And by virtue of the power, and for the purpose aforesaid, I do order and declare, that all persons held as slaves within said designated States, and parts of States, are and henceforward shall be free; and that the Executive Government of the United States, including the military and naval authorities thereof, will recognize and maintain the freedom of said persons. And I hereby enjoin upon the people so declared to be free to abstain from all violence, unless in necessary self-defence; and I recommend to them, that in all cases, when allowed, they labor faithfully for reasonable wages. And I further declare and make known, that such persons, of suitable condition, will be received into the armed service of the United States, to garrison forts, positions, stations, and other places, and to man vessels of all sorts in said service. And upon this act, sincerely believed to be an act of justice, warranted by the Constitution upon military necessity, I invoke the considerate judgment of mankind and the gracious favor of Almighty God.

In testimony whereof, I have hereunto set my name, and caused the seal of the United States to be affixed. — Done at the city of Washington, this first day of January, in the year of our Lord one thousand eight hundred and sixty-three, and of the independence of the United States the eighty-seventh.

ABRAHAM LINCOLN.

By the President:
WILLIAM H. SEWARD, *Secretary of State.*

1863. — PRINCIPAL EVENTS. — Gov. Andrew of Massachusetts takes the initiative in raising colored regiments in the free States. Gen. Banks, commanding the Department of the Gulf, orders that a whole army-corps be raised, eighteen regiments, to be called the "*Corps d'Afrique.*" In Virginia, Gen. Hooker supersedes Burnside in command of the Army of the Potomac, and is badly beaten at Chancellorsville, in May, by Lee. Gen. Meade supersedes Hooker, and overcomes Lee at Gettysburg July 1; and, July 4, Gen. Pemberton at Vicksburg surrenders to Gen. Grant. The country is filled with rejoicing. "Independence Day receives a new consecration." July 8, Gen. Gardner at Port Hudson surrenders to Gen. Banks. The Mississippi is opened its entire length, and the Confederacy is rent asunder. Other battles occur during the year, at Chickamauga, Chattanooga, Knoxville, &c. Three hundred thousand men are drafted. Riot in New York July 13. West Virginia admitted. A frightful massacre is perpetrated at Lawrence, Kan. The prominent rebel privateers of the year are "The Alabama" and "Florida."

1864. — The expedition to Meridan, the Fort-Pillow massacre, Red-River expedition, and Federal defeat at Olustee, Fla., occur between January and April. In March, 1864, Gen. Grant is placed in command of all the armies of the Union, with the rank of lieutenant-general. In May, he crosses the Rapidan with the army of the Potomac; and the battles of the Wilderness, Spottsylvania, North Anna, Cold Harbor, Petersburg, and Richmond, follow in quick succession. Gen. Sheridan drives the enemy from Maryland. Great victory at Winchester, — "twenty miles away." "In October," says Campbell, "the victory at Cedar Creek closes the war in the Shenandoah Valley."

Gen. William T. Sherman, May 6, commences a campaign resulting in his famous "march to the sea;" and terrific battles are fought at Chattanooga, Resaca, Dallas, Kenesaw Mountains, Atlanta, Fort McAllister, and Savannah, Ga. The privateer "Alabama" is sunk in the English Channel by the "Kearsarge," Capt. Winslow commanding. In August, Admiral Farragut wins a brilliant victory in Mobile Bay. Nevada is admitted. Abraham Lincoln is re-elected President.

1865.—Jan. 15. Fort Fisher, N.C., surrenders to Admiral Porter and Gen. Terry. In February, Gen. Sherman takes Columbia, S.C. Charleston is abandoned; and, on the 18th, Gilmore raises the stars and stripes over Fort Sumter. Gen. Canby and Admiral Thatcher take Mobile in April. Gen. Wilson is fighting in Alabama, Gen. Stoneman in South-western Virginia and North Carolina. Gen. Sheridan captures Early's army in the Shenandoah Valley, destroys the Richmond canal and railroad, and joins the army at Petersburg. March 9, Gen. Grant makes a final movement. April 1, Sheridan defeats Lee at Five-Forks Cross-Roads. April 2, Grant captures Petersburg; and, April 3, RICHMOND. April 9, Lee surrenders to Grant near Appomattox Court House. The loyal North is wild with enthusiasm. But, April 14, Pres. Lincoln is assassinated by a bold desperado named John Wilkes Booth; the Hon. William H. Seward, Secretary of State, is stabbed by another assassin; and the joy of the free States is soon hushed in deepest sorrow.

1865.— March 4. Extract from the last Inaugural Address of Pres. Lincoln : " With malice toward none, with charity for all, with firmness in the right as God gives us to see the right, let us strive on to finish the work we are in ; to bind up the nation's wounds; to care for him who shall have borne the battle, and for his widow and his orphans ; to do all which may achieve and cherish a just and a lasting peace among ourselves and with all nations. " ABRAHAM LINCOLN."

ANDREW JOHNSON.

1865. — April 15. Andrew Johnson, Vice-President, takes the oath as President. Gen. Johnston surrenders to Sherman. The assassin Booth, captured in a barn, refuses to surrender, and is shot. Other conspirators are hanged or imprisoned. Three hundred thousand Union men, and as many more Confederates, have been sacrificed to the Rebellion; hundreds of thousands are wounded; and the four-years' war is closed. Number of men furnished on both sides, from April, 1861, to June, 1865, 2,666,999. NATIONAL DEBT, $2,750,000,000.

Disagreements between Congress and the new President respecting the reconstruction of States recently in rebellion. Congress is pronounced by the President an illegal body, and its measures are repeatedly vetoed. Slavery is declared abolished by a three-fourths vote of the States. A Freedman's Bureau is established at Washington, under the charge of Gen. Howard. Jefferson Davis is captured, disguised in a woman's cloak and shawl, and sent to Fortress Monroe. The Southern Confederacy is at an end.

1866. — The Republican President affiliates with the Democratic party. Cabinet officers resign: Second Freedman's-Bureau Bill passed over the President's veto. Tennessee returns to the Union July 23. Emperor Louis Napoleon advises the United States that the French troops in Mexico, under Emperor Maximilian, are to be immediately withdrawn. Cyrus W. Field succeeds in laying the Atlantic cable between Europe and America. Telegraphic communication established.

1867.—By a two-thirds vote of both houses, Congress overrules the President's veto of the Reconstruction Bill, also the Tenure-of-office Bill and the District-of-Columbia Elective-Franchise Bill. All persons are now permitted to vote, without distinction of race or color. The loyal people sustain Congress, and denounce the President. In consequence of further vetoes of important measures, Mr. Ashley of Ohio moves the immediate impeachment of the President. The resolution is adopted, 137 to 38; forty-five not voting. Nebraska is admitted as a State. A national bankruptcy-law is passed. Alaska is purchased of Russia for seven million two hundred thousand dollars, gold.

1868.— Jan. 13. By vote of the Senate, Mr. Stanton returns to the Department of War, after temporary suspension by the President.

Feb. 21.—The President removes Mr. Stanton, and appoints Gen. Lorenzo Thomas *ad interim*. Congress objects, and Mr. Stanton remains. Feb. 22, the House votes, 126 to 47, that "Andrew Johnson, President of the United States, be impeached of high crimes and misdemeanors;" and articles of impeachment are accepted March 2. The Senate is convened as a court for the trial of the President, March 5; Chief Justice Salmon P. Chase presiding. Postponements follow. The trial commences March 30, and the case is submitted to the Senate May 6. On the 26th, the President is acquitted. Mr. Stanton resigns as Secretary of War. The Fourteenth Amendment to the Constitution is adopted by the necessary number of State legislatures, and the Fifteenth is suggested. The Pacific Railroad is in course of completion. Gen. Ulysses S. Grant is inaugurated President of the United States, and Schuyler Colfax Vice-President, March 4, 1869.

GRANT'S ADMINISTRATION.

1869 TO 1873.

THE CABINET.

PRESIDENT:
ULYSSES S. GRANT, Illinois.

VICE-PRESIDENT:
SCHUYLER COLFAX, Indiana.

SECRETARY OF STATE:
1869. — Hamilton Fish, New York.

SECRETARY OF THE TREASURY:
1869. — George S. Boutwell, Massachusetts.

SECRETARIES OF WAR:
1869. — John A. Rawlins, Illinois.
1869. — William W. Belknap, Iowa.

SECRETARIES OF THE NAVY:
1869. — Adolphe E. Borie, Pennsylvania.
1869. — George W. Robeson, New Jersey.

SECRETARIES OF THE INTERIOR:
1869. — J. D. Cox, Ohio.
1870. — Columbus Delano, Ohio.

POSTMASTER-GENERAL:
1869. — John A. J. Creswell, Maryland.

ATTORNEYS-GENERAL:
1869. — Ebenezer R. Hoar, Massachusetts.
1870. — Amos T. Akerman, Georgia.

CONTEMPORANEOUS ENGLISH HISTORY.

Reign. — Victoria.
Premier. — Mr. Gladstone.
Death of Lord Derby, Oct. 23, and George Peabody, Nov. 4, 1869.
Charles Dickens died June 9, 1870.
War between France and Prussia from July, 1870, to March, 1871.

APPENDIX.

PRESIDENTS OF THE CONTINENTAL CONGRESS,
From 1774 to 1788.

Peyton Randolph	Virginia	September	5, 1774.
Henry Middleton	South Carolina	October	22, 1774.
Peyton Randolph	Virginia	May	10, 1775.
John Hancock	Massachusetts	May	24, 1775.
Henry Laurens	South Carolina	November	1, 1777.
John Jay	New York	December	10, 1778.
Samuel Huntington	Connecticut	September	28, 1779.
Thomas McKean	Delaware	July	10, 1781.
John Hanson	Maryland	November	5, 1781.
Elias Boudinot	New Jersey	November	4, 1782.
Thomas Mifflin	Pennsylvania	November	3, 1783.
Richard Henry Lee	Virginia	November	30, 1784.
Nathaniel Gorham	Massachusetts	June	6, 1786.
Arthur St. Clair	Pennsylvania	February	2, 1787.
Cyrus Griffin	Virginia	January	22, 1788.

American Independence declared July 4, 1776.

Articles of Confederation adopted July 9, 1778.

The Constitution of the United States was ratified by the original thirteen States as follows:—

Delaware	December	7, 1787.
Pennsylvania	December	12, 1787.
New Jersey	December	18, 1787.
Georgia	January	2, 1788.
Connecticut	January	9, 1788.
Massachusetts	February	6, 1788.
Maryland	April	28, 1788.
South Carolina	May	23, 1788.
New Hampshire	June	21, 1788.
Virginia	June	26, 1788.
New York	July	26, 1788.
North Carolina	November	21, 1789.
Rhode Island	May	29, 1790.

PRESIDENTS OF THE UNITED STATES,

FROM 1789 TO 1871.

Name.	Born.	Died.	Age
George Washington,	Va., 1732,	Mt. Vernon, 1799,	67
John Adams,	Mass., 1735,	Quincy, July 4, 1826,	91
Thomas Jefferson,	Va., 1743,	Monticello, July 4, 1826,	83
James Madison,	Va., 1751,	Montpelier, 1836,	85
James Monroe,	Va., 1758,	New York, July 4, 1831,	73
John Quincy Adams,	Mass., 1767,	Washington, 1848,	81
Andrew Jackson,	N.C., 1767,	Hermitage, Tenn., 1845,	78
Martin Van Buren,	N.Y., 1782,	Kinderhook, 1862,	80
Wm. Henry Harrison,	Va., 1773.	Washington, 1841,	68
John Tyler,	Va., 1790,	Richmond, 1862,	72
James K. Polk,	N.C., 1795.	Nashville, Tenn., 1849,	54
Zachary Taylor,	Va., 1784,	Washington, 1850,	66
Millard Fillmore,	N.Y., 1800,		
Franklin Pierce,	N.H. 1804,	Concord, 1869,	65
James Buchanan,	Penn., 1791,	Wheatland, 1868,	77
Abraham Lincoln,	Ky., 1809,	Washington, 1865,	56
Andrew Johnson,	N.C., 1808,		
Ulysses S. Grant,	Ohio, 1822,		

SPEAKERS OF THE HOUSE OF REPRESENTATIVES,

FROM 1789 TO 1871.

1st Congress,	F. A. Muhlenberg	....	Pennsylvania.
2d	"	Jonathan Trumbull	Connecticut.
3d	"	F. A. Muhlenberg	Pennsylvania.
4th	"	Jonathan Dayton	New Jersey.
5th	"	{ " " .... "	
		{ George Dent	Maryland.
6th	"	Theodore Sedgwick	Massachusetts.
7th	"	Nathaniel Macon	North Carolina.
8th	"	" "	"
9th	"	" "	"
10th	"	Joseph B. Varnum	Massachusetts.
11th	"	" " "	"
12th	"	Henry Clay	Kentucky.
13th	"	{ " "	"
		{ Langdon Cheves	South Carolina.
14th	"	Henry Clay	Kentucky.
15th	"	" "	"
16th	"	{ " " .... "
		{ John W. Taylor	New York.
17th	"	P. P. Barbour	Virginia.
18th	"	Henry Clay	Kentucky.
19th	"	John W. Taylor	New York.
20th	"	Andrew Stevenson	Virginia.
21st	"	" "	"
22d	"	" "	"
23d	"	{ " " .... "
		{ Henry Hubbard	New Hampshire.
24th	"	John Bell	Tennessee.
25th	"	James K. Polk	"
26th	"	" " "	"
27th	"	R. M. T. Hunter	Virginia.
28th	"	{ John White	Kentucky.
		{ John W. Jones	Virginia.
		{ George W. Hopkins	"
29th	"	John W. Davis	Indiana.

30th Congress	{ Robert C. Winthrop ....Massachusetts.	
	Armested Burt...................South Carolina.	
31st	"	Howell Cobb......................Georgia.
32d	"	Linn Boyd........................Kentucky.
33d	"	" " ...."
34th	"	Nathaniel P. Banks...............Massachusetts.
35th	"	James L. Orr ....South Carolina.
36th	"	William Pennington ....New Jersey.
37th	"	Galusha A. Grow..................Pennsylvania.
38th	"	Schuyler Colfax..................Indiana.
39th	"	" " ...."
40th	"	" " ...."
41st	"	James G. Blaine..................Maine.
42d	"	" " " ...."

CHIEF JUSTICES OF THE UNITED-STATES SUPREME COURT, 1789–1871.

John Jay. ....New York.............September 26, 1789.
John Rutledge ....South Carolina..........July   1, 1795.
   (Ratification refused by the Senate.)
William Cushing........Massachusetts ....January   27, 1796.
   (Appointment declined.)
Oliver Ellsworth ....Connecticut ....March   4, 1796.
John Jay ....New York..............December 19, 1800.
   (Appointment declined.)
John Marshall........ Virginia ....January   31, 1801.
Roger B. Taney........Maryland ....December 28, 1835.
Salmon P. Chase.......Ohio....................December 6, 1864.

ADMINISTRATIONS FINANCIALLY.

OFFICIAL FIGURES OF THE EXPORTS, IMPORTS, EXPENDITURES, AND DEBT OF THE UNITED STATES.

Washington's Administration.

Year.	Exports.	Imports.	Expenditures.	Debt.
1789	....	....	....	....
1790	$20,205,156	$23,000,000	....	....
1791	19,012,041	29,200,000	$7,207,539	$75,463,476
1792	20,753,098	31,500,000	9,141.569	77,227.924
1793	26,109,572	31,000,000	7,529,575	80,352.634
1794	33,026,233	34,600,000	9,302.124	78,427,400
1795	47,989,472	69,756,268	10,405,069	80,747,587
1796	67,064.097	81,436,164	8,367.776	83,762,172

John Adams's Administration.

1797	56,850,206	75,379,406	8,626,012	82,064 479
1798	61,527,097	68,551,700	8,613,507	79,228 529
1799	78,665,522	79,089,148	11,077,043	78,408,669
1800	70,970,780	91,252,768	11,989,739	82,976,291

Jefferson's Administration.

1801	94,115,925	111,363,511	12,273,376	82,038,050
1802	72,483,160	76,333,333	13,276,084	80,712,632
1803	55,800,038	64,666,666	11,258,983	77,054,686
1804	77,699,074	185,000,000	12,624,646	86,427,120
1805	95,566,021	120,600,000	13,727,124	82,312.150
1806	101,536,963	129,410,000	15,070,093	75,723,270
1807	108,343.151	138,500,000	11,292,292	69,218,398
1808	22,430,960	56,990 000	16,764,584	65,196,317

Madison's Administration.

1809	52,203,333	59,400,000	13,867,226	57,023,192
1810	66,657,970	85,406,000	13,319,986	53,178,217
1811	61,316.883	53,400,000	13,601.808	48,005,587
1812	38,527,236	77,030,000	22,279,121	45,209,737
1813	27,855,927	22,005,000	39,190,520	55,962,827
1814	6,927,441	12,965,000	38,028,230	81,487.846
1815	52,557,753	113,041,274	39,582,493	99,833,660
1816	81,920.452	147,103,000	48,244,495	127,334,933

Appendix.

Monroe's Administration.

Year.	Exports.	Imports.	Expenditures.	Debt.
1817	$87,671,560	$99,250,000	$40,877,646	$123,491,965
1818	93,281,133	121,750,000	35,164,875	103,466,633
1819	70,141,501	87,125,000	24,004,199	95,529,648
1820	69,661,669	74,450,000	21,763,024	91,015,566
1821	64,974,382	62,585,724	19,090,572	89,987,427
1822	72,160,281	83,241,541	17,676,592	93,546,676
1823	74,699,030	77,579,267	15,314,171	90,875,877
1824	75,986,657	89,549,007	31,898,538	90,269,777

John Quincy Adams's Administration.

Year.	Exports.	Imports.	Expenditures.	Debt.
1825	99,535,388	96,340,075	23,585,804	83,788,432
1826	77,595,322	84,974,477	24,103,398	81,054,059
1827	82,324,727	79,484,068	22,656,764	73,987,357
1828	72,264,686	88,509,824	25,459,479	67,475,043

Jackson's Administration.

Year.	Exports.	Imports.	Expenditures.	Debt.
1829	72,358,671	74,492,527	25,044,358	58,421,413
1830	73,849,508	70,876,920	24,585,281	48,565,406
1831	81,310,583	103,191,124	30,038,446	39,124,191
1832	87,176,943	101,029,266	34,356,698	24,322,235
1833	90,140,443	108,118,311	24,257,298	7,001,032
1834	104,336,973	126,521,332	24,601,982	4,760,081
1835	121,693,577	149,895,742	27,573,141	351,289
1836	128,663,040	189,980,085	30,934,664	291,089

Van Buren's Administration.

Year.	Exports.	Imports.	Expenditures.	Debt.
1837	117,419,376	140,989,217	37,265,037	1,878,223
1838	108,486,616	113,717,404	39,455,438	4,857,660
1839	121,088,416	162,092,132	37,614,936	11,983,737
1840	132,085,936	107,641,519	28,226,553	5,125,077

Harrison and Tyler's Administration.

Year.	Exports.	Imports.	Expenditures.	Debt.
1841	121,851,803	127,946,177	31,787,530	6,737,398
1842	104,691,531	100,152,087	32,936,876	15,028,486
1843*	84,346,480	64,753,799	12,118,105	27,203,450
1844	111,200,046	108,435,035	33,642,010	24,748,188

Polk's Administration.

Year.	Exports.	Imports.	Expenditures.	Debt.
1845	114,646,606	117,254,564	30,490,408	17,093,794
1846	113,488,516	121,691,707	27,632,282	16,750,926
1847	158,648,622	146,545,638	60,520,851	38,926,623
1848	154,032,131	154,998,928	60,655,143	48,526,870

* To June 30.

Appendix.

Taylor and Fillmore's Administration.

Year.	Exports.	Imports.	Expenditures.	Debt.
1849	$145,755,820	$147,857.439	$56,386,422	$64,704,693
1850	151,898,790	178,138,318	44,604,718	64,228,238
1851	218,388,011	216,224,932	48,476,104	62,560,395
1852	209,658,366	212,945,442	46,712,608	65,130,692

Pierce's Administration.

1853	230,976,157	267,978,647	54,577,061	67,340,628
1854	278,241,064	304,562,381	75,473,119	47,242,206
1855	275,156,846	261,468,520	66,164,775	39,969,731
1856	326,964,908	314,639,943	72,726,341	30,963,900

Buchanan's Administration.

1857	362,960,608	360,890,141	71,274,587	29,060,386
1858	324,644,421	282,613,150	82,062,186	44,910,777
1859	356,789,461	338,768,130	83,678,643	58,754,699
1860	400,122,296	362,162,541	77,055,125	64,769,703

Lincoln's Administration.

1861	243,971,277	286,598,135	85,387,313	90,867,828
1862	229,938,985	275,357,051	570,841,700	514,211,371
1863	322,359,254	252,919,920	805,796,630	1,098,796,181
1864	301,984,561	329,562,895	1,298,144,656	1,740,690,489

Johnson's Administration.

1865	336,697,123	234,339,810	1,897,674,224	2,682,593,026
1866	550,684,299	445,512,158	1,141,072,666	2,783,425,879
1867	438,577,312	411,733,309	1,093,079,655	2,692,199,215
1868	454,301,713	373,409,448	1,069,889,970	2,636,320,964

PUBLIC DEBT OF THE UNITED STATES, FROM JULY 31, 1865, TO MARCH 1, 1871.

	Maximum War Debt, July 31, 1865.	Debt at Close of Last Admin., March 1, 1869.	Present Outstanding Debt, March 1, 1871.
Five-twenty six-per-cent stock	$606,569,500	$1,602,587,350	$1,424,098,300
Other six-per-cent stock	302,301,042	283,677,400	283,678,100
Ten-forty five-per-cent stock	172,770,100	194,567,300	194,567,300
Other five-per-cent stock	27,022,000	27,022,000	20,000,000
Three-year 7.30-per-cent notes	830,000,000	......	......
Three-year six-per-cent notes	212,121,470	......	......
Total funded	$2,150,784,112	$2,107,854,050	$1,922,343,700
Greenback notes	$473,114,799	$356,021,073	$356,100,186
Greenback certificates	205,822,845	71,140,000	55,238,000
Gold certificates	......	28,775,560	20,657,500
Fractional currency	25,750,032	36,781,547	40,573,748
Past-due notes and bonds	17,263,120	6,422,464	3,261,112
Total treasury circulation	$721,950,796	$499,140,644	$484,830,546
Less gold in treasury	35,337,858	98,741,261	103,174,290
Less currency balance	$686,612,938	$400,399,383	$381,656,357
	81,401,775	16,853,529	20,854,606
Net treasury circulation	$605,211,163	$383,545,854	$360,801,731
Total principal of debt	$2,755,995,275	$2,491,399,904	$2,283,145,431
Yearly interest, in gold	$64,419,628	$124,255,550	$113,194,949
Yearly interest, in currency	87,412,423	2,134,200	1,657,140
Total amount of interest charge	$151,832,051	$126,389,550	$114,852,089

Appendix.

TREASURY DEPARTMENT OF THE UNITED STATES.
SECRETARIES FROM 1789 TO 1869.

1789. Alexander Hamilton..................New York.
1795. Oliver Wolcott, jun..................Connecticut.
1800. Samuel Dexter......................Massachusetts.
1802. Albert Gallatin.....................Pennsylvania.
1814. G. W. Campbell....................Tennessee.
1814. A. J. Dallas........................Pennsylvania.
1817. W. H. Crawford ....Georgia.
1825. Richard Rush......................Pennsylvania.
1829. Samuel D. Ingham..................Pennsylvania.
1831. Louis McLane......................Delaware.
1833. W. J. Duane.......................Pennsylvania.
1833. Roger B. Taney....................Maryland.
1834. Levi Woodbury....................New Hampshire.
1841. Thomas Ewing ....Ohio.
1841. Walter Forward...................Pennsylvania.
1843. John C. Spencer...................New York.
1844. George M. Bibb....................Kentucky.
1845. R. J. Walker......................Mississippi.
1849. W. M. Meredith..................Pennsylvania.
1850. Thomas Corwin...................Ohio.
1853. James Guthrie....................Kentucky.
1857. Howell Cobb......................Georgia.
1860. Philip F. Thomas..................Maryland.
1861. John A. Dix......................New York.
1861. Salmon P. Chase...................Ohio.
1864. W. P. Fessenden...................Maine.
1865. Hugh McCulloch..................Indiana.
1869. George S. Boutwell................Massachusetts.

POPULATION OF THE UNITED STATES.

CENSUS, 1870.

States.	Population.	States.	Population.
Alabama	996,988	Nebraska	123,000
Arkansas	483,179	Nevada	42,491
California	560,285	New Hampshire	318,300
Connecticut	537.418	New Jersey	905,794
Delaware	125,015	New York	4,382,834
Florida	187,751	North Carolina	1,069,401
Georgia	1,195,077	Ohio	2,662,333
Illinois	2,539,638	Oregon	90,922
Indiana	1,673,941	Pennsylvania	3,519.601
Iowa	1,191,720	Rhode Island	217,356
Kansas	362,872	South Carolina	728.000
Kentucky	1,321,001	Tennessee	1,258,288
Louisiana	727,050	Texas	797,500
Maine	626,463	Vermont	330,552
Maryland	780,894	Virginia	1,224,947
Massachusetts	1,457,351	West Virginia	442,032
Michigan	1,184,296	Wisconsin	1,055,167
Minnesota	435,511		
Mississippi	834,170	Total of States	38,086,396
Missouri	1,717,258		

Districts and Territories.	Population.
District of Columbia	131,706
Arizona	9,658
Colorado	39,706
Dakotah	14,181
Idaho	14,998
Montana	20,594
New Mexico	91,852
Utah	86,786
Washington	23,901
Wyoming	9,118
Total	442,500
Total States	38,086,396
Total United States	38,528,896

POPULATION OF THE UNITED STATES.

	1790.	1800.	1810.	1820.	1830.	1840.	1850.	1860.	1870.
Whites	3,172,464	4,304,489	5,862,004	7,861,937	10,537,378	14,195,605	19,553,068	26,957,471	
Free Colored	59,466	108,395	186,446	238,150	319,599	386,303	434,495	532,090	
Slaves	697,897	893,041	1,191,364	1,538,038	2,009,043	2,487,455	3,204,313	3,953,760	
Total	3,929,827	5,305,925	7,239,814	9,638,131	12,866,020	17,069,453	23,191,876	31,443,321	38,528,896

Area of the United States, including Alaska, nearly four million square miles.

THE TWENTY MOST POPULOUS CITIES IN THE UNITED STATES.

No.	Cities.	1870.	1860.	Per Cent.
1.	New York	922,531	805,658	14.6
2.	Philadelphia	674,022	565,529	19.2
3.	Brooklyn	306,309	206,661	48.7
4.	St. Louis	310,864	160,773	93.4
5.	Chicago	293,983	109,260	173.7
6.	Baltimore	267,354	212,411	25.9
7.	Boston	250,526	177,840	40.9
8.	Cincinnati	216,239	161,044	34.3
9.	New Orleans	191,322	168,675	13.5
10.	San Francisco	149,482	56,802	163.2
11.	Buffalo	117,715	81,129	45.1
12.	Washington	109,204	61,122	78.8
13.	Newark	105,078	71,941	43.1
14.	Louisville	100,753	68,033	48.1
15.	Cleveland	92,846	43,417	113.9
16.	Pittsburg	86,235	49,217	75.3
17.	Jersey City	81,744	29,226	179.7
18.	Detroit	79,580	45,619	74.5
19.	Milwaukie	71,499	45,246	58.1
20.	Albany	69,422	62,367	11.4

IMMIGRATION.

From Ireland to America, from May, 1847, to January, 1869,		1,597,805
" Germany " " " "		1,536,649
" England " " " "		498,578
" Scotland " " " "		100,595
" France " " " "		74,405
" Switzerland " " " "		62,608
All other countries " " " "		168,351
	Total,	4,038,991

THIRTEENTH, FOURTEENTH, AND FIFTEENTH AMENDMENTS TO THE CONSTITUTION OF THE UNITED STATES.

1865. — ARTICLE XIII., *Section 1.* — Neither slavery nor involuntary servitude, except as a punishment for crime, whereof the party shall have been duly convicted, shall exist within the United States, or any place subject to their jurisdiction.

Sect. 2. — Congress shall have power to enforce this article by appropriate legislation.

1868 — ARTICLE XIV., *Section 1.* — All persons born or naturalized in the United States, and subject to the jurisdiction thereof, are citizens of the United States, and of the State wherein they reside. No State shall make or enforce any law which shall abridge the privileges or immunities of citizens of the United States; nor shall any State deprive any person of life, liberty, or property, without due process of law, nor deny to any person within its jurisdiction the equal protection of the laws.

Sect. 2. — Representatives shall be apportioned among the several States according to their respective numbers, counting the whole number of persons in each State, excluding Indians not taxed. But when the right to vote at any election for the choice of electors for President and Vice-President of the United States, representatives in Congress, the executive and judicial officers of a State, or the members of the legislature thereof, is denied to any of the male inhabitants of such State, being twenty-one years of age, and citizens of the United States, or in any way abridged, except for participation in rebellion or other crime, the basis of representation therein shall be reduced in the proportion which the number of such male citizens shall bear to the whole number of male citizens twenty-one years of age in such State.

Sect. 3. — No person shall be a senator or representative in Congress, or elector of President and Vice-President, or hold any office, civil or military, under the United States, or under any State, who, having previously taken an oath as a member of Congress, or as an officer of the United States, or as a member of any State legislature, or as an executive or judicial officer of any State, to support the Constitution of the United States, shall have engaged in insurrection or rebellion against the same, or given aid or comfort to the enemies thereof. But Congress may, by a vote of two-thirds of each House, remove such disability.

Sect. 4 — The validity of the public debt of the United States, authorized by law, including debts incurred for payment of pensions and bounties for services in suppressing insurrection or rebellion, shall not be questioned. But neither the United States, nor any State, shall assume or pay any debt or obligation incurred in aid of insurrection or rebellion against the United States, or any claim for the loss or emancipation of any slave; but all such debts, obligations, and claims, shall be held illegal and void.

Sect. 5. — That Congress shall have power to enforce by appropriate legislation the provisions of this article.

1870. — ARTICLE XV., *Section* 1. — The right of citizens of the United States to vote shall not be denied or abridged by the United States, or by any State, on account of race, color, or previous condition of servitude.

Sect. 2. — Congress shall have power to enforce this article by appropriate legislation.

www.ingramcontent.com/pod-product-compliance
Lightning Source LLC
Chambersburg PA
CBHW031813230426
43669CB00009B/1125